The Psychology of Preventive Health

The current social and political climate places increasing emphasis on the prevention of ill health. Health promotions and campaigns try to persuade individuals to adopt healthy lifestyles and eschew unhealthy habits. From her extensive experience in health psychology **Marian Pitts** provides an overview of the latest research in the area of preventive health and questions some underlying assumptions in current practice. She also asks whether psychologists have a role to play in this fast developing area. *The Psychology of Preventive Health* is illustrated with examples of current practice in the National Health Service in Britain and the health services of other nations. It will prove essential reading for students and health professionals interested in widening their perspectives on issues concerning primary health care.

Marian Pitts is currently Professor of Psychology and Head of the Division of Psychology at Staffordshire University. Previously she has worked in Africa and taught at the Universities of East London, Tennessee and Zimbabwe. She is co-editor of *The Psychology of Health* (1991).

The Psychology of
Preventive Health

Marian Pitts

London and New York

First published 1996
by Routledge
11 New Fetter Lane, London EC4P 4EE

Simultaneously published in the USA and Canada
by Routledge
29 West 35th Street, New York, NY 10001

Routledge is an International Thomson Publishing Company

© 1996 Marian Pitts

Typeset in Bembo by LaserScript, Mitcham, Surrey
Printed and bound in Great Britain by
Redwood Books, Trowbridge, Wiltshire

British Library Cataloguing in Publication Data
A catalogue record for this book is available from the British Library

Library of Congress Cataloging in Publication Data
A catalogue record for this book has been requested

ISBN 0–415–10682–6 (hbk)
ISBN 0–415–10683–4 (pbk)

Contents

List of figures

Acknowledgements

I would like to extend my warm thanks to Helen Jackson and to Dr Fred Jackson who provided useful information, most especially concerning HIV/AIDS, and to Linda McGowan for her help in tracing source material. Thanks are also due to librarians at the North Staffordshire Medical Institute and Staffordshire University. Christine Burton offered much appreciated secretarial support and Doreen Thompson worked on the index. Anne Southall knew the words and has the spirit of a cockeyed optimist.

I am especially mindful of my debt to colleagues at Staffordshire University who have offered advice and information on subjects as diverse as bicycle helmets and how many measures there are in a bottle of whisky. The errors in all matters are, unfortunately, my own.

Finally, and especially, my thanks go to my family, who were there when they were needed and were absent when it helped.

For Mum, who has known both health and illness

Chapter 1

What is preventive health?

INTRODUCTION

It is customary to begin introductory chapters with a definition of the subject matter and an indication of the scope of what will be discussed. I will follow this tradition. Preventive health seeks to understand the origins of common diseases and to devise strategies to tackle them before they affect individuals adversely. The World Health Organisation defines health as: '. . . a state of complete physical, mental and social well-being and not merely the absence of disease or infirmity'. (WHO, 1946). A study of health then, inevitably considers economic, social, cultural, political and environmental factors as they have impact on our daily lives.

Rose begins his book on *The Strategy for Preventive Health* by stating that: 'Few diseases are the inescapable lot of humanity, for a problem that is common in one place will usually prove to be rare somewhere else' (Rose, 1992: 1). He cites rates of cervical cancer and infant mortality statistics as indicators of the wide differences in patterns of health and disease: 'There is no known biological reason why every population should not be as healthy as the best.' (ibid.) Prevention in this context really means delaying death. Everyone dies, and for our purposes everyone has to die of something. As Marmot and Mustard point out 'The total number of deaths cannot change – one per person.' (1994: 213). The aim of much preventive health therefore is to substitute an early death, say before the age of 60 years in the UK, for a later one. We will return to this issue in later chapters, but for now the aim is clear – to improve the lot of all people by reducing the threats to their health.

Underlying this aim is the supposition that we all want good health. This may seem so far beyond dispute that it would seem inappropriate to pause even for a moment to consider the veracity of this position. However, very few of us, in fact, experience optimal health for any period of time. A distinction between being healthy and being sick is not always easy to make. When was the last time you felt completely free of aches, pains, or niggling symptoms such as a blocked nose or itchy feet? The answer is likely to depend on your age I suspect; but the fact is that surveys regularly show that the majority of us are experiencing such minor symptoms most of the time. In addition, many of us regularly over-indulge in many ways that we know are likely not only to damage our long-term health, but also, and often more pressingly, to make us feel awful in a very few hours' time. Wellness and illness form a continuum with optimal health at one end, some neutral point in the middle perhaps, and then a continuum of 'illness' from minor signs of ill health, through symptoms to disability and premature death. Preventive health is concerned with keeping people to the 'wellness' end of the model, or, at the very least, slowing the slide through signs and symptoms to major disabling conditions. We can, and often do, exercise choice in the matter.

The value of optimal health to us may not be as high as we automatically assume. We will encounter ideas of cost–benefit analysis throughout this book; do the benefits of good health outweigh the costs? This question has meaning on a number of levels, including an analysis of the short-term ratio as well as a long-term one. When I began this book I encountered a statement by the writer John Mortimer that summarises for me the dilemma of preventive health research: 'There is no human activity, eating, sleeping, drinking or sex, which some doctor, some where, won't discover leads directly to cardiac arrest' (Mortimer, 1978). We may not all share Mortimer's views on life and death, but the ideas behind his statement may resonate. If everything one does is potentially harmful to health, then what is the point of abstaining from any of it ? The toast when my glass is full is still to 'good health'!

In the United Kingdom preventive health has received increasing attention from health professionals and from government. The publication of *The Health of the Nation* (DoH, 1992a) has stimulated debate about what can and can't be done, on behalf of and in the name of people. *The Health of the Nation* sets out agendas and targets for actions in health care until the end of this century. It has developed a strategy that selected the five areas of coronary heart disease and stroke, cancers, mental illness, HIV/AIDS and sexual health and accidents as ones where substantial improvements in health could be achieved. For each area it set targets such as:

- To reduce the consumption of cigarettes by at least 40 per cent by the year 2000 (from 98 billion manufactured cigarettes per year in 1990 to 59 billion in 2000).

- To reduce the rate of conceptions amongst the under 16s by at least 50 per cent in the year 2000 (from 9.5 per 1,000 girls aged 13–15 in 1989 to no more than 4.8).

There is a clear economic argument that can be made for preventive health care measures such as these. Reducing the incidence of a disease ought, in theory, to save money. In practice the economic argument is a weak one – people not dying early means they live longer, and during those extra years of life are likely to cost more in their utilisation of health care services than they contribute by the fruits of their labours. Rose (1992) estimates that somewhere around the age of 50 is the balance point where the benefits of more productive years are outweighed by the additional costs of surviving into old age. If we were to follow a strictly economic argument we would be unlikely to direct resources at preventing those diseases that carry us off in late middle age.

I am not seriously advancing an argument for the early disposal of elderly unproductive members of the community; that would be wicked. The point I wish to make here is that the justifications for promoting good health by preventing disease are moral, not economic. As Rose states unequivocally: 'It is better to be healthy than ill or dead. That is the beginning and the end of the only real argument for preventive medicine. It is sufficient' (Rose, 1992: 5). Health psychology's role in prevention is a crucial one. Most preventive strategies work on the principle of change. Change has to be achieved either by an individual changing a 'risk behaviour', or by an agency making a change to circumstances, placing guards around dangerous machinery, for example. Psychologists are experts in understanding how change occurs and it is their models of change that we will go on to consider. First though we need to return to the concepts of health and illness and our perceptions of them.

PREVENTIVE HEALTH BEHAVIOURS

Underlying much of the research in health psychology is the concept of a health behaviour, or a preventive health behaviour (PHB). These are behaviours undertaken by people to enhance or maintain their health. There are innumerable instances of PHBs: the daily cleaning of teeth, wearing of seat belts, reducing fat and sugar in one's diet, or pumping iron are a few examples.

The value of PHBs was provided by a much cited study carried out in Alameda County, California and reported initially by Belloc and Breslow

(1972). They asked 6,928 county residents which of the following seven health behaviours they practised regularly:

- not smoking
- having breakfast each day
- having no more than one or two alcoholic drinks each day
- taking regular exercise
- sleeping 7 to 8 hours per night
- not eating between meals
- being no more than 10 per cent overweight.

They also measured the residents' health status via a number of illness related questions – how many days they had had off from work due to sickness in the previous twelve months, for example. They included five indices concerned with mental health and they designed a measure of social health which they defined as 'the degree to which individuals were functioning members of their community'. There are a number of criticisms that could be made of this study, most notably the lack of independence between the questions; however, some fairly strong and often replicated relationships were demonstrated. Adults who engaged in *most* of the health habits reported themselves to be healthier than those who engaged in *few* or *none*. A health habit is a health behaviour that is well established and often carried out semi-automatically – do you actually decide each morning and evening to clean your teeth or do you just do it? A follow-up study nine and a half years later showed that mortality rates were significantly lower for both men and women who practised the seven healthy habits. Men who had seven healthy habits had only 23 per cent of the mortality rate of men who had between zero and three health habits (Breslow and Enstrom, 1980). There was a clear link between physical and mental health, and social health was also found to be associated with physical health. These findings reinforce the notion of health as a composite of effective functioning physically, mentally and socially. However, it is the effectiveness of health habits that most directly concerns us here.

This original Californian cohort has now been studied for twenty-five years with two follow-up surveys and many follow ups of mortality. The survey in 1982, seventeen years after the study first began, considered those persons who were at least 60 years old at the time of the first survey. It was found that smoking, physical activity and regular breakfast eating were strong predictors of their mortality. Note that it was the absence of the first habit and the presence of the other two that predicted longevity.

The Alameda Study reinforced the idea of 'moderation in all things' as the basis of good health. It also emphasised the role of social and mental aspects in achieving good physical health.

The dilemma or challenge then is how best to encourage, persuade or coerce people into adopting the healthy habits that it is believed are good for them. I hope the value-laden aspects of this enterprise are already apparent. The dilemma for health psychologists is to explain why some or many people don't do what they know is in their own best interests to do; and why some people are more amenable to the adoption of healthy habits than others.

INDIVIDUAL DIFFERENCES AND HEALTH BEHAVIOURS

Lay beliefs

The extent to which people feel in control of their health is likely to be related to, amongst other things, their theories about disease causation and prevention (Calnan, 1987). These theories can have a variety of sources: some could be characterised as biomedical in origin and nature of explanation, whilst others are 'lay' in that their source is not medical. Frequently lay and biomedical beliefs concerning particular diseases are held in parallel. It is rarely the case that a single set of 'scientifically established' beliefs comes to replace lay beliefs as an individual gains new knowledge about a disease. Rather, beliefs come to be held conjointly.

Cancer is one of the diseases that has attracted greatest research interest in this area. Sontag (1979) suggested that cancer is the disease that is most feared in industrial societies, although AIDS now comes close in the fear it provokes. Blaxter (1983) and Linn *et al.* (1982) examined lay beliefs about the causes and prevention of cancer within specific groups such as working-class grandmothers and cancer patients. Calnan (1987) examined lay perspectives and emphasised that, in the case of cancer, it is particularly difficult to develop clear conceptual frameworks that under-lie either the scientific or the lay beliefs about causation. His study of women's beliefs identified smoking as a major factor for them, with biological predisposition and some form of hereditary theory also figuring large. There was also an idea of 'a trigger' – something that provokes an inborn predisposition. Many people feel that nothing can be done to avoid cancer and this has obvious implications for attempts to prevent the disease. In Calnan's study, working-class women were particularly likely to regard the disease as unavoidable 'if your number comes up'.

Middle-class women were more likely to identify behavioural factors such as smoking as linked to risk. Fallowfield (1991) lists a number of lay beliefs of causal factors in breast cancer. The most frequently cited causal factor was a knock or injury; others cited 'stress' as a causative factor. Some women attribute the development of cancer to a previous infection and even imply that it may be contagious. Fallowfield quotes a cancer sufferer who says: 'I'd been working as a cleaner at an old people's home and lots of them died of cancer. I suppose I could have picked something up there, couldn't I?' (Fallowfield, 1991: 21). The implications of beliefs such as these, both for the cancer sufferer and those around her are clear.

Very little psychological research has been carried out on lay beliefs about health in developing countries. This is an important area of concern; increasingly it is recognised that health education within a country can be effective only if it is framed within a context that is appropriate to that country (Pearson, 1986; Wall, 1988). Anthropological studies of belief systems, of which there have been many since Rivers outlined his major categories of illness causation in 1924, have tended not to focus on specific diseases or relate their findings directly to health education programmes. Stainton Rogers (1991) usefully outlines a number of approaches to the study of medical beliefs systems. She draws attention to 'medical pluralism' where alternative medical systems are studied to ascertain how they co-exist and compete with each other within a cultural context. Medical systems are classified, for example, as exogenous (outside the person) or endogenous (within the person). A recent study by Elliott *et al.* (1992) examined nurses' beliefs about parasuicide as predictors of their behaviour towards patients following suicide attempts. They found that both traditional and biomedical beliefs were held in parallel and that the combination was predictive of behaviour. Lay beliefs have close links with how an illness is cognitively represented, and these elements will be considered shortly in relation to models of health behaviour.

Over the past fifteen years there have been numerous attempts to identify 'personality types' or 'cognitive types' who differ in their likelihood of adopting health behaviours. I will not try to list every difference that has been considered. Instead, I will choose two or three that indicate the kinds of research questions posed by this work and the range of results obtained.

Health locus of control

In the mid 1960s the concept of 'locus of control' was introduced by Rotter and others (Rotter, 1966). This grew out of a social learning tradition that considered the expectations of individuals and how they related to reinforcements. Individuals with an internal locus of control were more likely to believe that reinforcements were contingent upon their own efforts, whereas those with an external locus of control were likely to regard their life as determined largely by external forces such as fate or 'powerful others'. In the context of health behaviours, it was found that those who had an 'internal locus of control' more likely to engage in a range of health behaviours: wearing seat belts, stopping smoking and using contraception, for example (Pitts and Phillips, 1991).

A development of this broad construct of locus of control was the Health Locus of Control scale constructed by Wallston et al. (1978). Questions reflected the three factors mentioned above: an internal focus for health 'I am in control of my health'; the powerful others factor 'Whenever I don't feel well I should consult a health professional'; and the role of fate 'Luck plays a big part in determining how soon I will recover from an illness.' There is some evidence (reviewed by Wallston and Wallston in 1984) that high 'internal scorers' carried out a greater range and number of health behaviours; but differences between internals and externals are not particularly large, and the amount of variance accounted for by this measure is frequently small (Pitts et al., 1991). Furnham and Steele (1993) review locus of control questionnaires, including those for health. There have been a number of disease-specific questionnaires developed: Bradley et al., for example, have considered locus of control in relation to diabetes (Bradley et al., 1984, 1990); others have applied the approach to cancer (Pruyn et al., 1988), and to hypertension (Stanton, 1987). Furnham and Steele point out that the critical practical issue for further research is whether locus of control beliefs can be altered by interventions. Many researchers make the point that the aim of devising a scale is to identify those people who hold maladaptive beliefs. Very little, however, has developed from these identifications.

Self-efficacy

Bandura, again from a social learning perspective, has suggested that self-efficacy is a major factor to be considered in accounting for differences in health behaviours (Bandura, 1977, 1986). It has been applied to helping people quit smoking and to persuading people to indulge in physical exercise. It examines people's beliefs in their own abilities with questions such as: 'Am I confident I could deal efficiently with unexpected events?', or 'Can I always manage to solve difficult problems if

I try hard enough?'. It has been studied both as a behaviour specific to a narrow situation and as a more general trait construct.

The model has also recently been applied to condom use by Wulfert and Wan (1993). They developed an outline of a model that places self-efficacy as a common pathway which integrating the effects of several cognitive variables that might predict condom use. The first of these variables is sexual attitudes, the second is outcome expectancies, i.e. what would be the effect of using a condom. Comparison and influences from a peer group were seen as important, as were knowledge and perceived vulnerability about AIDS.

The results from this study support the role of self-efficacy as a mediating variable between factors such as peer influence, knowledge and perceived vulnerability and an actual behaviour. A note of caution should be sounded here. The study was essentially a correlational one and there is therefore no direct evidence from it that self-efficacy actually *causes* increased condom use. Such studies have prompted attempts to enhance self-efficacy beliefs, especially amongst young adults.

Optimism

Schwarzer (1994) identifies two kinds of bias that may affect our perception of vulnerability, as expressed in the Health Belief Model, to be considered later in this chapter. These are a temporal comparison bias and a social comparison bias. The first occurs when someone links two events that are independent; this distortion is known as the Monte Carlo error and is exemplified by the belief that 'lightning never strikes twice'. It occurs most when the events are rare – I have won the national lottery once therefore it is impossible for me to win it again (why would one try?). The second kind of bias involves comparison with others. Questions about one's own risk are compared with answers to questions about the risks of others similar to the target person: 'Compared with others of my age, my chances of developing . . . are greater than/the same as/less than them.' The usual response is to judge oneself at less risk of almost anything than one's contemporaries. It appears that most people engage in this social comparison bias with regard to many health issues such as risks of lung cancer, AIDS and heart disease. There is also evidence that this kind of optimism is particularly characteristic of adolescence where it is known as 'adolescent invulnerability'. These biases are dysfunctional in terms of health behaviours and health promotion. They are likely to act as defence strategies against behavioural change. Other kinds of optimism, however, are more adaptive because they imply coping strategies and behavioural change. Researchers such as Scheier and Carver (1992) have shown that optimists have better health and practise more health behaviours than pessimists; this is possibly linked to the fact that optimists expect good outcomes and hence cope better with short-term distress or discomfort. The links between optimism and self-efficacy are close; each construct is measured by questionnaires that are rarely unidimensional.

Wallston (1994) has offered an interesting distinction between 'cautious' and 'cockeyed' optimism. The cautious optimist is 'pretty much in touch with reality'; being fairly confident that things will turn out right, the person nevertheless does everything in his or her power to ensure that it does. The 'cockeyed optimist' — in the words of Rogers and Hammerstein — is 'stuck like a dope with this thing called hope', lives in a world of illusion and hardly raises a finger to help bring about the desired outcome. In the context of health care this results in little change towards healthy habits and avoiding unhealthy ones. Given this, one would predict a curvilinear relationship between optimism and health behaviours with only the cautious optimism items predicting uptake and maintenance of health behaviour.

It should be apparent that the constructs outlined above have much in common: they emphasise effort and self-belief as key constructs in predicting health behaviours. Many of these elements have been combined to create models that can explain and predict patterns of health behaviours. It is in the quest for explanatory models of health behaviours that we are now engaged.

MODELS OF HEALTH BEHAVIOUR

The Health Belief Model

This model, probably the most influential in health psychology, has been with us now for a long time. It was first proposed by Rosenstock (1966) and was developed and modified by Becker and Maiman (1975). It attempts to explain the adoption of health behaviours. It suggests that the readiness to take preventive health action is a function of a number of dimensions. The person must:

- feel personally susceptible to the disease (perceived susceptibility)
- feel that the disease would have at least moderately serious consequences (perceived severity)

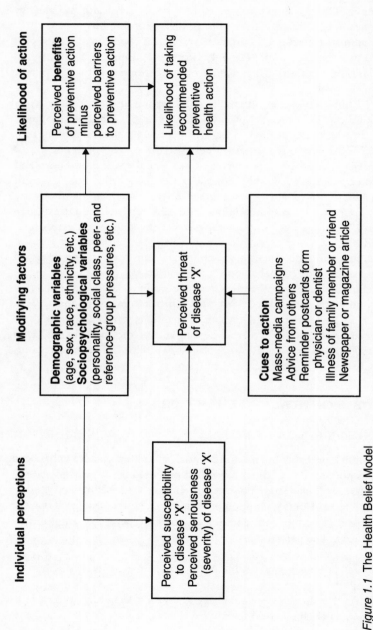

Figure 1.1 The Health Belief Model

Source: Becker and Maiman, 1975

- feel that the preventive health behaviour would be beneficial either by preventing the disease or reducing the severity of its impact (perceived benefits)
- feel that the estimates of physical, psychological, financial and other costs are outweighed by the benefits resulting from adopting the health behaviour.

There is evidence now from a large number of published studies that the Health Belief Model (HBM) can successfully predict different health behaviours. In their review of the model in 1984, Janz and Becker found support for the four elements – susceptibility, severity, benefits and barriers – in both retrospective and prospective designs. In particular, they identified the dimension of 'perceived barriers' as the major determinant in the model.

More recently, Harrison *et al.* (1992) carried out a meta analysis of studies using the HBM. They identified 147 studies using the HBM, but could analyse only 16 of them due to their stringent inclusion criteria that required that, amongst other criteria: the data were collected from adults, the four variables of the model were all measured and that actual behaviour was tested rather than a report of attitude or intention. The model did not fare well. Ten per cent was the largest amount of variance accounted for by the dimensions in any study. Retrospective studies using the HBM found significantly higher effect sizes for benefits and costs, and a lower mean for severity. Few studies were prospective in design. One major problem is that there is rarely confirmation for the full model; rather, different elements are seen to be important for different health behaviours.

Studies on intentions to use condoms in Zimbabwe carried out by David Wilson and his associates have reported that the HBM accounted for only 15 per cent of the variance associated with intended condom use by men and 12 per cent for women (Wilson *et al.*, 1990). Most worryingly, the variables contributing significantly to each of these equations were different. In other words, different elements of the model seemed to be predictive of condom use for men respondents than for women. Clearly this is a problem and the choice of condom use highlights the dilemma. Using a condom during sexual intercourse is, obviously, a health behaviour involving two persons; we need to understand both persons' motivations and, preferably, how they interact.

There are also serious problems with the reliability and validity of the measures used in studies of HBM. Frequently, questions are designed for each study, with very little check on test retest reliability and somewhat scant evidence of the link between the questions and the behaviours being studied.

Breast screening and self-examination are areas where a large body of research has been carried out using the HBM as its theoretical basis. Here the picture is less gloomy in terms of the model's success. Calnan (1984) reviewed studies of HBM applied to breast cancer. He considered the health belief variables to be the best predictors, for example, of attendance for screening. However, once again the amount of variance accounted for by the model rarely rises above 15 per cent. The issues associated with screening are discussed further in Chapter 3. In practice, we find it extremely difficult using the HBM to predict with any degree of certainty who will, or will not, engage in a health behaviour; and what aids or hinders the process of adoption and maintenance of such health behaviours.

The Theory of Reasoned Action

The Theory of Reasoned Action and its later development the Theory of Planned Behaviour are more formally specified social cognition models. The models have as their central premise that people make decisions about their behaviour on the basis of a reasonable consideration of the available evidence. The Theory of Planned Behaviour (TPB) means what it says in that behaviour is planned and that the planning is in part a function of an individual's intentions. Intention is a key construct in these models. Intention is described by Fishbein as follows:

> If one really wanted to know whether someone would or would not perform a given behaviour, the simplest and probably the most efficient thing one could do was to ask that person whether he or she was or was not going to perform that behaviour. And, as one might expect, people turn out to be very good predictors of their own behaviour.
>
> (Fishbein, 1993: 9)

Intention is determined by three sets of factors: the attitude towards the behaviour, the subjective norm (the perceived social pressure towards performing the specified behaviour), and the perceived control over the behaviour.

Terry *et al.* (1993) show how they operationally define these elements in their studies of condom use. Intention is measured by items such as 'I intend to use a condom on my next sexual encounter'. Attitude is measured by: 'Using a condom on my next sexual encounter would be . . .'; subjective norm is measured by 'People who are important to me think that I should/should not use a condom on my next sexual

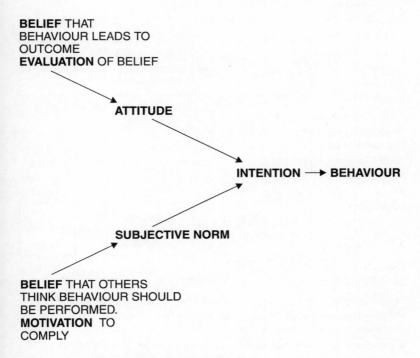

Figure 1.2 The Theory of Reasoned Action

encounter'. Perceived control is measured by 'For me to use a condom on my next sexual encounter would be easy/difficult.'

There are two stages to this model and questions to be asked at each stage. The first stage is whether these three sets of factors of attitudes, subjective norms and perceived control do in practice predict the intention to perform a particular behaviour. The second question is whether intention to perform a behaviour accurately predicts actual performance. Continuing with the example of condom use outlined above the single most important predictive variable tends to be the availability of a condom, i.e. having one in one's pocket at the time of the next sexual encounter.

Illness Representation Model

There has been an increasing recognition that the way in which individuals *think* about their health and health concerns may have a direct impact on their health behaviours. The Illness Representation Model

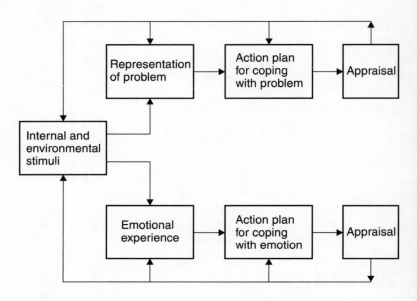

Figure 1.3 The Self-Regulatory Illness Representation Model
Source: Leventhal and Cameron, 1987

developed by Leventhal and his colleagues seeks to reflect these representational aspects (Leventhal and Cameron, 1987).

The model is a self-regulatory one since this conceptualises the individual as an active problem-solver who attempts to move from his or her current position to his or her desired state and who appraises success or failure at every stage. The model identifies three stages as important: cognitive representation, action planning or coping, and appraisal. First the individual identifies what is wrong ('I am getting too fat'), then develops a plan ('I will cut down on my calorie intake') and then appraises the effects ('I have cut down except for the occasional chocolate bar').

Illness representations have been studied in a variety of ways. Jenkins (1966) used factor analysis on sixteen questions related to illness: severity, susceptibility and preventability, for example. He identified three dimensions that he thought underlie the representations of all diseases: personal involvement, human mastery and social desirability. These results have been criticised since then (Croyle and Barger, 1993), although the basis of illness representation has not changed markedly. People differ in the degree to which they are 'symptom aware'. Pennebaker (1982) has studied individual differences in symptom perception and has shown that social circumstances as well as internal states can influence both the perception, identification and response to symptoms. The 'storehouse' of knowledge of symptoms, causes and preventive actions of illness underpin the ways in which a current bodily state is interpreted.

Protection Motivation Model

Rogers (1984) examined health behaviours from the point of view of motivational factors. The protection motivation model suggests that motivation to protect oneself from a health threat is based on four beliefs:

1 that the threat is severe (magnitude)
2 that one is vulnerable to the threat (likelihood)
3 that one can perform the behaviour required to protect against threat (self-efficacy)
4 that the response will be effective (response efficacy).

Early research emphasised fear as a motivational factor but Rogers now suggests instead that attempts need to be directed at all four of the elements described above to achieve effective change. It is not clear which of the four elements are more important than the others nor how to develop a campaign that can adequately address all elements simultaneously.

The Transtheoretical Model

The Transtheoretical Model has been developed by Prochaska and DiClemente (1983, 1992) as an integrative and comprehensive model of behaviour change. They suggest that people move through a series of stages of change which they label precontemplation, contemplation, preparation, action and maintenance. Using studies on how people stop smoking as an example, the stages would be like this:

- *Precontemplation*: a period during which a smoker is not considering giving up (say for the next six months)
- *Contemplation*: a period during which a smoker is seriously considering quitting
- *Preparation*: a period during which a smoker seriously thinks about giving up, say during the next month
- *Action*: a period ranging from nought to six months during which a smoker has actually stopped smoking
- *Maintenance*: a period beginning six months after a smoker has ceased to smoke and during which time he or she continues not to smoke.

Thus the model is temporal and describes the process of change rather than only identifying the precursors to that behavioural change. The decision–making element associated with the model derives from Janis and Mann's (1977) conflict model which involves a consideration of benefits and costs (pros and cons) associated with a behavioural change.

Prochaska *et al.* (1994b) applied the stages of change to twelve problem behaviours, which included: smoking cessation, weight control, quitting cocaine, using condoms, using sunscreens, and others. Twelve separate samples were drawn on for each of the problem behaviours yielding a total sample size of 3,858. Looking at costs and benefits of behavioural change, the study showed that for all twelve problem behaviours, the cons of changing were higher than the pros for those subjects in the precontemplation stage. The opposite was true for those subjects in the action stage. For seven of the twelve behaviours the crossover in the balance between pros and cons occurred during the contemplation stage, for the other five behaviours it was during the action stage.

Prochaska *et al.* (1994a) review studies on the Transtheoretical Model of change and HIV prevention and concluded that the model is generalisable to HIV prevention. They highlight the importance of distinguishing between main sexual partners and casual sexual partners and suggest different factors are operating in decisions to use condoms with these two groups. We will consider studies such as these in more detail in Chapter 6.

The Precaution Adoption Process

Weinstein has recently developed a model which he calls the Precaution Adoption Process (1988). He identifies five stages that an individual moves through to adopt a healthy behaviour. These are:

1   has heard of the hazard
2   believes others are susceptible to the hazard
3   acknowledges personal susceptibility to the hazard
4   decides to take action against the hazard
5   takes precautions.

(Weinstein 1988: 356)

The key elements of Weinstein's approach are the acknowledgement that knowledge alone is insufficient for change and that significant others can influence one's own recognition of personal susceptibility.

Which model works?

Weinstein compares some of these models in a review article in 1993 in which he tries to identify key questions to be asked of any theory that aims to improve our understanding of health protective behaviour. Some of these questions are:

- to what extent do beliefs about the likelihood and severity of health outcomes combine to influence behaviour? Are their effects additive, multiplicative or what?
- how important are perceptions of risk compared to other non-risk issues?
- do doubts about one's ability to carry out a precaution have a different impact on behaviour than other obstacles?
- what variables intervene between intentions and actions?
- what attributes of precautions other than beliefs about costs and effectiveness affect our behaviour?

(Weinstein 1993: 332)

Social cognition models have had a positive effect generally on our understanding of the factors that can be important in developing and changing people's health behaviours. However, there are a number of problems with this group of models as a whole. Perhaps the most important criticism is that their focus is on the individual. No matter how many extraneous variables are added to the accounts, they still assume the individual as the central focus. For us as psychologists this is perhaps appropriate, but one only has to look at the history of social and medical advances to realise that policy and public measures, such as ensuring clean drinking water, can have a vital role in achieving good health. If one's drinking water is polluted, then no amount of 'healthy eating' on the part of an individual could compensate. These wider issues will be discussed throughout the book but will be reconsidered especially in the last chapter.

Other problems with these models are discussed in a paper by Bennett *et al.* (1995). They suggest that there are serious shortcomings to social cognition approaches to health. These are that such models tend to neglect routine or non-cognitively mediated health behaviours, and that much health behaviour happens routinely. In other words, the models tend to over-emphasise health behaviours and under-emphasise healthy habits. Bennett *et al.* report a qualitative study of middle-aged adults' food choices that showed that much of their eating was determined by habit which was rarely consciously considered. Many of us have regular timetables of meals – the Sunday roast, fish and chips on a Friday and so on; and many of us are on 'automatic pilot' when whizzing around the supermarket for the weekly shopping. If I had to make a decision on each item, the shopping trip could last a whole morning.

Bennett *et al.* offer as a contrast to social cognition models something which might be called a social–contextual model, in other words, a model which emphasises the 'wider context' in which health behaviours are occurring. As Ground points out in a witty parody of the debate:

> If we took into account that . . . people are pretty complicated, then we could be more effective. We have to see that people are neither just rational decision makers, nor just black boxes responding to external stimuli but are a bit of both with a whole lot more complicated, and more important stuff thrown in too.
>
> (Ground 1995: 25)

The issues raised in this chapter will recur throughout the book. Each chapter that follows will consider a different aspect of preventive health. The book does not cover all relevant aspects, and in some cases only the briefest overview has been possible. However, I hope that the approaches and methodologies that are introduced here can be applied to other issues which are not dealt with in this book. I hope also to show that psychologists can have a key role to play in the challenges of enhancing health and preventing disease.

Chapter 2

Vaccination

INTRODUCTION

The development and employment of vaccines has had a dramatic effect, world-wide, on the incidence of infectious diseases. Early childhood illnesses, in particular, have virtually been eradicated in the United Kingdom by the implementation of a national policy of childhood vaccinations. Nevertheless, there is still a shortfall in the take up rates advocated by governments. If we take an example from the UK then we see that the target for major childhood vaccinations recommended before the age of 2 years is 95 per cent. There is, then, a small but significant proportion of the population – parents, professionals and others – who do not take their children for vaccination, and/or who argue strongly against their widespread use. Psychologists have had remarkably little to say about this preventive health behaviour. This chapter will review psychological studies to date and consider ways in which future studies could be of interest and importance in the field of vaccination.

First though, we need to understand what vaccination is and what a vaccine does. A vaccination is a procedure whereby immunity to an infection is achieved, whether by inducing it actively or passively. Active immunity is induced by 'using inactivated or attenuated live organisms or their products' (DoH, 1992b). Live attenuated vaccines are those such as polio, rubella, mumps and measles. Bacterial and viral vaccines contain killed or inactivated components such as injectable polio vaccine, or those for hepatitis A and B. Most vaccines achieve their effect by stimulating the production of antibodies, often more than one injection of the vaccine is needed to achieve a high number of antibodies; although some, such as the vaccines for rubella and measles, achieve immunity after a single dose. Passive immunity can be achieved from the injection of human immunoglobin: this has immediate; but relatively short-lasting effects and is mainly used for immunosuppressed individuals, or those under immediate threat of a disease.

Vaccines can be administered orally, as normally nowadays in the case of polio; via an intramuscular injection (most vaccines), or intradermally, as in the case of BCG for tuberculosis. Thus, we can see already that there are a number of ways in which vaccines and vaccinations differ, and some of these differences may be of psychological significance.

The recommended schedule of routine immunisation for children in the United Kingdom is as follows:

Early childhood vaccines
- Diphtheria, tetanus and pertussis (DTP), polio, Hib
  First dose at two months, second at three months and third at four months.
- Measles, mumps and rubella (MMR)
  twelve to eighteen months

Later childhood vaccinations
- Booster DT and polio
  four to five years
- Rubella (girls only)
  ten to fourteen years
- BCG
  ten to fourteen years (or infancy)
- Booster tetanus and polio
  fifteen to eighteen years

Thus, the average child in the UK should have received the following vaccines: three doses of DTP, Hib and polio by six months old; measles, mumps and rubella by fifteen months a fourth DTP and polio by school entry; a BCG and a rubella (for girls) by fourteen years, and a fifth polio and tetanus by school-leaving age. Most children have therefore received approximately fifteen vaccinations, with eleven of them being in the form of injection. This does not include special initiatives such as the recent measles campaign for all school-aged children.

VACCINATION – A SUCCESS STORY?

Lochhead summarises the success of vaccination in the UK as follows: 'In the case of diphtheria, immunisation has brought about a dramatic reduction in the incidence of the disease and it is now extremely rare' (Lochhead 1991: 130). From 1986 to 1991 there were only 13 cases of diphtheria notified, with no deaths. Approximately 20 cases of tetanus occur annually with a 20 per cent mortality rate (four people). These occur mostly in unimmunised adults.

Poliomyelitis is also extremely rare today, following the introduction of an effective vaccine. The move from the early intradermal injection to a liquid form of vaccination that could be administered orally has undoubtedly made the vaccination more attractive. The decrease in polio cases in the United Kingdom has been from around 2,800 notifiable cases each year, with 326 associated deaths, down to three cases only in 1988, of which two were 'vaccine associated' and one acquired overseas. The notion of 'vaccine associated' cases is an important one. Because the oral polio vaccine is live, recipients can excrete the vaccine virus; this can place others at a small risk of contracting the virus if they are in some way susceptible to it. In Germany, this risk was estimated at five per million cases. This risk could be greater if the immune system was suppressed for any reason. In Zimbabwe, only one child has died from polio in the last year. No child in England or Wales died of acute measles–related illness in either 1990 or 1991. In 1991 there were only 12,000 cases of measles. An expected measles epidemic was reported to have been averted in 1994/5 following a national immunisation campaign directed at school children. The campaign involved about seven million children and cost £200 million; the costs and benefits of this exercise are hard to judge. It is anticipated that mumps will be eliminated shortly if current levels of immunisation are maintained. In 1991 in the UK there were 2,924 cases of mumps.

From statistics such as these we might conclude that the story of vaccination is one of continued success. This is not entirely the case, however. There is some evidence that 'non-compliance' with the vaccine programme is increasing within the countries of the West. The World Health Organisation has a target of near universal vaccination to be achieved by the year 2000. It seems that this is unlikely to be met, since even in Western countries such targets are not yet achieved. In the United States, vaccine rates have altered recently (Freed et al., 1993). Between 1989 and 1990 there was a 52 per cent increase in the number of reported measles cases, and the incidence of infectious rubella has increased 500 per cent since 1988 (Lee et al., 1992). Freed et al. also report that the early childhood immunisation programmes of the United States compare poorly with other countries. In 1991 sixteen other countries had immunisation rates for children under one year old that were higher than the US. These countries included Bulgaria, Brazil, Greece, Romania and Chile. WHO reported in 1990 that Asia has a higher rate of immunisation of 1 year olds (86 per cent) than either Europe (80 per cent) or the Americas (82 per cent). A 1990 target in the UK of 90 per cent primary immunisation for all children under the age of 2 years was not achieved (Bennett and Smith, 1992). Bobo *et al.* (1993) analysed data from a population based sample of 1,163 children in the states of Oregon and Washington. They report that only 60 per cent of the children in their sample had received the recommended full series of immunisations by their second birthday. Furthermore, only 40 per cent of children of poorly educated mothers, 45 per cent of children of single mothers and 55 per cent of those who were not first-born were fully up-to-date with their vaccination programme.

WHO CHOOSES NOT TO VACCINATE?

Bennett and Smith (1992) sampled a cohort of children in Mid Glamorgan between the ages of 2 and 2½ years. They obtained data on the vaccination status of each child. From this, 300 children were identified of whom one-third had received all pertussis vaccinations, one-third had an incomplete record of pertussis vaccinations, and one-third had had refused the pertussis vaccination refused for them by their parents. Primary care-givers of these children were interviewed and data were obtained on their attitudes and beliefs concerning vaccination. Those parents who had refused the pertussis vaccination reported signi-ficantly more concern over their child experiencing long-term health problems as a result of the pertussis vaccination than parents of children who were fully vaccinated. The non-vaccination group also reported higher concern over the risk associated with the MMR (measles, mumps and rubella) vaccination than did the fully vaccinated group. Neither of these results should surprise us, and it is important to note that parents of children who had received the full vaccination programme were likely to be less anxious about risks, perhaps because their own children had successfully previously passed the 'risk period' immediately post vacci-nation, or they may have been less anxious generally about vaccinations. Overall, Bennett and Smith report a lower perceived benefit from the vaccination for the non-vaccinated group than for the fully vaccinated group. Parents of the non-vaccinated group of children also valued the pertussis and MMR vaccinations less.

Other aspects of this study are also interesting. More than half the parents interviewed had delayed a vaccination for their child at some time. More than half the parents of non-vaccinated children reported that they had seen their child distressed after a previous vaccination and found this worrying and important; and nearly one-fifth reported un-sympathetic treatment by clinic staff as a factor in their decision not to vaccinate. In summary:

> Those who do not vaccinate their children appear to have a degree of both anxiety concerning the risks and to underestimate the potential benefits of vaccination. They may also be reacting to some negative experiences related to the process of vaccination itself.
>
> (Bennett and Smith 1992: 347)

Discussion of perceived benefits and risks leads us inevitably to a consideration of the Health Belief Model. Several studies of vaccinations have reported results in the framework of this model. Major variables reported are perceived severity of the disease, perceived susceptibility to the disease, and sources of information concerning vaccination. Per-ceived severity of the disease has been addressed in a number of studies, often indirectly. Dalphinis (1986) found, in a small sample of mothers, that 52 per cent knew nothing about diphtheria, 42 per cent knew nothing about tetanus, and 39 per cent about polio. Forty nine per cent did not think whooping cough (pertussis) was a serious disease, and 77 per cent had the same view regarding measles. Reid (1987), in a large cohort study in Liverpool, also reported poor understanding of measles and whooping cough. Roden (1992) considered the importance of knowledge gained from personal experience. He found that very few parents in a sample from the Western suburbs of Australia had known anyone with diphtheria (4 per cent) or tetanus (10 per cent). Twenty-nine per cent had seen people with polio and 38 per cent had seen people with whooping cough. We do not have equivalent percentages for the UK, but in all probability the percentages could be even lower. Thus, it would seem that perceived severity is low for many of the childhood diseases currently controlled by vaccination. It is ironic that the success of the vaccination programme means that the majority of parents prob-ably have not had direct contact or personal experience of the diseases discussed here. Their information, therefore, must of necessity be in-direct and second-hand, often coming only from formal information sources such as leaflets.

Bennett and Smith (1992) considered perceived importance of the pertussis vaccination and reported that the parents of the non-vaccinated children rated the importance of the vaccination significantly lower than the other parents. Blair et al. (1985) drew attention to the fact that as many as 63 per cent of parents in their sample thought that immunisation was only sometimes, if ever, effective. It has been suggested that the fact that immunised children can still contract the disease, even if the effects are less severe, is regarded by parents as evidence that the vaccination 'doesn't work'. In fact, in the case of the pertussis vaccination, immunity is conferred on around 80 per cent of recipients.

Recently, a study of children who had not received immunisation found that over one-fifth of parents cited homeopathy as the reason for not immunising their children (Simpson *et al.*, 1995). They quote examples of the replies from parents such as: 'I use homeopathy to protect my child and I am confident that this is the best way of doing so.' Many homeopaths also believe that the potential long-term damage that live vaccines may cause is too great a risk to take. Religious reasons accounted for 16 per cent of refusals: 'my child is protected but not by immunisation. We are Christian Scientists'; 'My children . . . are protected by God's promise not by man's vaccination.'. Reasons which might broadly be described as 'medical' accounted for only 5 per cent of the reasons. The authors suggest an 'immunisation hotline' might be a way of enabling concerned parents to discuss the issue of immunisation promptly and confidentially. We have to recognise, however, that there is always likely to be a small proportion of children who are *not* vaccinated because of parents' beliefs.

Research by Reading *et al.* (1994) investigated whether an intervention designed to improve overall immunisation uptake affected the social inequalities associated with uptake. All children born in the county of Northumberland in four birth cohorts between 1981 and 1991 were examined for uptake of measles, pertussis and diphtheria immunisation. Although coverage increased substantially over the period for all vaccinations, inequalities between deprived and affluent areas of the county at the very least persisted and, in some cases, increased.

PSYCHOSOCIAL VARIABLES AND VACCINATION

Studies in less-developed countries have tended to consider demographic and geographic variables rather more than psychological ones. Zeitlyn *et al.* (1992) cite mothers' education as the single most important determinant of childhood vaccination in Bangladesh. Zondag and Voorhoeve (1992) confirm the link between maternal education and children's successful vaccination in three rural areas in Zambia. The link seems less apparent in the West. Rosenblum *et al.* (1981) reported 'no difference between compliant and non-compliant subjects on ethnicity, age, income, religion or education'. Other studies (Mitchell, 1985 and Green, 1970), have found the same relationship described in the above studies. Access to clinics has also been shown to be important both in less-developed countries such as Zambia (Zondag *et al.*, 1992 and Pillai and Conaway, 1992) and in countries such as the United States (Freed *et al.*, 1993), the United Kingdom (Senior *et al.*, 1990) and Australia (Roden, 1992).

If it is the case that few parents have had direct personal experience of the childhood diseases covered by vaccination programmes, it is important to investigate other potential sources of information on vaccination, and to consider their role in achieving compliance with recommended vaccination schedules. New and Senior (1991) asked mothers in north-west England where they had received their advice about immunisation. Health visitors were the chief advisers for around 55 per cent of mothers, relatives also provided advice to around 52 per cent. New and Senior report differences between those mothers of children who had completed the pertussis course of vaccinations and those who were incomplete. Incomplete immunisers had received less advice and help from health professionals and were far less likely to have received information in the form of leaflets about immunisation. They were more likely than complete immunisers to have received advice from friends. The link between types of advice received and maternal education is probably important here. Health leaflets are sometimes difficult to read and understand. A 1993 leaflet on Hib (*A Parents' Guide to the New Hib Immunisation*) begins:

> Hib is a bacterium (a type of germ) which can infect young children causing . . . meningitis – an illness in which the lining of the brain becomes swollen . . . Hib can also cause another illness – epiglottis – a severe swelling of the throat which can be fatal.

The leaflet goes on to refer to septicaemia, pneumonia and infections of bones and joints. Whilst stating quite clearly the benefits of Hib, there is little that is easily understood in the discussion of meningitis. It may well be that complete immunisers are better educated than incomplete immunisers, and hence would be more likely to read and understand leaflets such as that described above.

Reid (1987) suggested that the influence of non-health professionals was more likely to be negative than positive. Reid, reported in Lochhead, 1991, states that amongst those who consented to pertussis vaccination, the greatest influence was the husband (51 per cent), whilst those who refused the pertussis vaccination were most influenced positively by the maternal grandmother (20 per cent) and negatively by the husband (37 per cent). The explanation of the husband's influence, and the determinants of the direction of that influence are unspecified and undetermined. New and Senior's research emphasises that, regardless of the level of professional advice received, mothers were most influenced by a range of past experiences and lay advice.

A RATIONAL CASE FOR REFUSING VACCINATION

New and Senior's study (1991) was one of few qualitative studies into the uptake of infant immunisations. They are also among the few researchers who seem prepared to consider that there might be a rational case for non-vaccination. They found that many mothers, both of complete and incompletely immunised children, had thought about the process and debated it extensively. Several mothers recounted negative incidences during previous vaccinations. For example, one mother had an eldest son who had developed an allergic reaction to his first injection; she had been assured that there would be no negative consequences to the injection and so was now suspicious of health professionals' advice. Four other mothers also cited distressing side effects in older children: one child had suffered hair loss, another had received one injection too many as a result of a lost record card. Others cited that fact that children who had received the whooping cough vaccination had, nevertheless, gone on to contract whooping cough. They concluded 'immunisation was therefore, in their opinion, a pointless exercise.' An interesting fact on information sources and influence that relates to the discussion earlier is that at least 35 out of 123 full immunisers had seen a case of whooping cough.

A study by Keane et al. (1993) used focus groups in Baltimore to examine attitudes towards vaccine efficacy, illness and health. They found that vaccines were considered to be only partially effective; susceptibility to chicken pox was often cited as evidence that vaccination failed. Vaccines were also seen to cause fever, which was regarded as a cardinal indicator of illness; hence vaccines were perceived to be *causing* illness rather than preventing it. Diseases such as diphtheria, whooping cough, polio and measles were regarded as lower threats to children's health than drugs, street violence and being with 'the wrong crowd'. Again, the lack of direct experience of the severity of these childhood diseases seems to lead to a reduction in the perception of their threat to health and life.

A number of studies have identified lack of knowledge among health professionals as a hindrance to vaccination. Lochhead (1991) reports a study by Nichol and Ross (1985) that examined health visitors' knowledge of risk factors for immunisation. Thirty-eight out of forty were unsure whether current antibiotic treatment would render a vaccination unsafe or ineffective. Given the high number of infants who receive antibiotics, such uncertainty is of obvious concern. A study by Klein *et al.* (1989) examined 173 children for their history of immunisation. They found uptake of immunisation was 89 per cent for diphtheria, tetanus and polio, 64 per cent for pertussis and 64 per cent for measles. One hundred and six children were incompletely vaccinated, of which 38 per cent were the result of two false contra-indications: a temporary intercurrent infection and a history of atopy. Inappropriate advice was just as likely to have come from a general practitioner as from a health visitor or health clinic. They concluded that immunisation was still viewed as 'a potential hazard that should be avoided if some excuse could be found'. This view was held not just by parents, but also by health professionals. Reddy (1989) carried out a similar study in West Sussex. He sampled non-attenders for measles, mumps and rubella vaccinations and found that common reasons for non-attendance were that the child was unwell at the time of appointment or that appointments were forgotten or at an inconvenient time. On investigation, the unwell children had simple colds without any systemic upset and would therefore have been considered fit for vaccination. Reddy also comments that parents were not alone in their uncertainties when a child had a minor illness: 'this uncertainty was also shared by reception staff in the surgery' (Reddy 1989: 739).

Hewitt (1989) followed up a cohort of 522 school-age children. He found that inaccurate contra-indications were present in 13.4 per cent for the pertussis vaccination and 7.5 per cent for the measles vaccination. Inaccurate reasons given by parents for omitting the pertussis vaccination were 'fits in distant relatives', a family history of atopy, mental retardation in a relative, and admission to neonatal intensive care. Only twelve (2.3 per cent) children would have been excluded from the pertussis vaccination according to current guidelines.

Pilgrim and Rogers (1995) raise a number of ethical doubts for primary health care workers. They consider mass childhood immunisation as driven by propaganda rather than by a free flow of information; they bemoan the absence of a no-fault compensation policy which they consider also militates against a free debate about risks; and they consider a clash of imperatives between the pressure on health professionals to pursue population targets against the rights of parents to object to immunisation. Their paper may well open up the debate again about the value of immunisation for the community and for the individual. Certainly, at the time of writing this, it would seem that for a parent to choose to immunise a child against polio in the UK is little more than an altruistic gesture, necessary nonetheless.

ESTIMATING AND UNDERSTANDING RISKS

An area of research that has a clear link with research on vaccination uptake is that of risk perception. There is now a substantial literature that investigates people's understandings of relative risks and the factors which may influence them. As Fischoff *et al.* (1993) point out in a recent review of risk perception and communication, there is a common complaint from experts that 'lay people simply do not realise how small (or large) the risk is.' The implication of this is that it would be relatively easy to redress this problem by conveying accurate information to 'lay people'. However, the problem is not so easily solved. The use of verbal quantifiers such as 'quite likely' or 'rare' can be extremely problematic in health communications. An example given in Fischoff's review is to compare 'likely to be fatal' with 'likely to rain'. This example conveys well the different meanings of the same word. Fischoff *et al.* also caution against the assumption that experts and lay people share definitions of risk. Such difficulties make it unlikely that information given is guaranteed to improve understandings of risk. Very little work has considered the importance of the 'target' of the risk estimate. For example, I may estimate what would be an acceptable risk to myself rather differently from what I would consider to be an acceptable risk to my child, parent, or workforce. A study by Quadrel *et al.* (1993) addressed the contentious issue of adolescent invulnerability. Unfortunately, it did not consider the acceptability of risk as opposed to the likelihood of a risky event occurring. Such considerations make the efficacy of statements about risk, of the kind often found in immunisation leaflets, difficult to assess.

ADULT VACCINATION PROGRAMMES

Not all vaccinations occur during childhood of course, although a quick glance at the literature would suggest as much. Vaccinations of adults tend to be of three types: work-related precautions, such as vaccination against hepatitis B, which is now routine amongst police officers, health workers and paramedics, vaccinations for 'at risk groups', such as flu jabs for the elderly, and vaccinations for travel overseas.

Department of Health Guidelines recommend vaccination against hepatitis B for those who might be at increased risk because of 'occupation, lifestyle or other factors such as close contact with a case or carrier' (DoH, 1992b: 113). 'High risk' occupations are mainly in the health care professions where personnel have direct contact with blood or blood-stained body fluids, or tissue. Compliance with such recommendations is relatively low. Kinnersley (1990) carried out a postal survey of general practitioners who were asked whether they thought it a good ideas for GPs to be vaccinated against hepatitis B, whether they themselves had been vaccinated, and if not, why not. Of the 598 GPs who replied to the survey, 528 (88 per cent) believed all GPs should be vaccinated, but only 287 (48 per cent) had been vaccinated themselves. Reasons for not having the vaccine were: 'I just have not got round to it' (81 per cent), 'I am at very low risk' (13 per cent), whilst only three GPs said they did not trust the vaccine, and only four said the vaccination was of no proven benefit. Kinnersley concludes: 'General practitioners may not need to be vaccinated against Hepatitis B, but the discrepancy between their belief that they do and the prevalence of vaccination needs addressing' (Kinnersley, 1990: 238).

Downing (1993) reports a study on maternity staff at an East London hospital. She considered awareness and knowledge of viral hepatitis B infection and vaccination status. She found that staff under-estimated the prevalence of viral hepatitis B by a factor of two, that 70 per cent had had a needle stick injury during their career, and 50 per cent had had at least one in the past twelve months. Seventy per cent of the sample were fully immunised. All paediatricians in the sample were immunised, and more midwives than obstetricians were fully immunised. Of those not fully immunised, obstetricians were more likely to be partly immunised whilst midwives were more likely not to have had immunisation at all. The main reason for failing to achieve full immunisation was 'apathy'. So, once more we see the gap between intention and behaviour, even within such relatively well informed groups as health professionals.

THE GREAT FLU EPIDEMIC

In the autumn of 1993 there was a flurry of newspaper articles concerning a predicted flu epidemic. Comparisons were made with the winter of 1989/1990 when it was reported that between 19,000 and 25,000 people died of influenza. The newspaper reports (*Guardian* 27/10/93, *Independent* 5/11/93) focused on a shortage of flu vaccines to avoid such deaths. A number of statistics were given to indicate the severity of the risk.

> Influenza like illnesses should normally run at about 40 cases per 100,000 population at this time of year. Last week however the figure was 67 and this week 127 cases per 100,000 population were being recorded. . . . The 1989 epidemic peaked . . . at 580 cases per 100,000 population, about 550,000 cases in the worst week.
>
> (*Guardian*, 27/10/93)

Here we see, in the course of one paragraph, a number of comparative statistics being offered to express a magnitude of increased risk. We have little idea how people would compute risk from the combination of figures offered them. If we add to this the fact that the flu vaccine being discussed was considered by Professor John Oxford, Head of Virology at the Royal London Hospital, to offer around 70 per cent protection we can begin to appreciate the complexities of estimating the value or need for a 'flu jab'. No further newspaper articles emerged and the headline of 'Flu sweeps south as epidemic fears grow' appears to have been unfounded.

An interesting study by Gene *et al.* (1992) considered attitudes towards influenza immunisation in Barcelona, Spain. They surveyed, by telephone, 190 patients at high risk for influenza (usually because of age or another medical condition). Factors that predicted uptake of the flu vaccine were self-identification as being at high risk, and belief that the immunisation itself would not cause discomfort. Those who did not agree to the vaccination thought themselves less susceptible to the illness and doubted the effectiveness of the vaccine. They also cited conflicting information from the mass media. There seems to be some problem in achieving appropriate identification of oneself as at risk of the illness. The models discussed in Chapter 1 all emphasise the importance of perceived susceptibility in the process of adopting a health behaviour.

Stehr-Green *et al.* (1990) interviewed by telephone, in the United States, 9,851 people over the age of 65, of whom 32 per cent reported having been vaccinated against influenza in the past twelve months. They found no differences in vaccination coverage based on gender, education level or household income. White respondents were significantly more likely to have been vaccinated than either Black or Hispanic respondents. People who were obese, did not regularly use seatbelts when driving, and who were current smokers, were all less likely to have received a vaccination. The characteristic most strongly associated with vaccination, though, was that those who had had a medical examination within the preceding year were twice as likely to have had a vaccination than those who had not had a check up. Stehr-Green *et al.* emphasise that a recommendation by a health care provider would seem to be an extremely effective way of implementing recommended vaccinations for some adults.

There seems a paucity of work that considers travellers and their need for vaccination. The World Health Organisation has specific guidelines for recommended vaccinations for travellers to many different parts of the world, but unfortunately there is little research on the uptake and on the psychosocial aspects of such vaccinations.

CONCLUSIONS

What then can we conclude about the psychosocial aspects of vaccination? First, that there is a clear link between knowledge of an illness and the likelihood of vaccination. Second, that demographic variables are just as important in understanding Western patterns of immunisation as they are in 'less developed' countries. Third, risk perceptions, especially on behalf of others, are also important determinants of immunisation uptake and these perceptions will be strongly influenced by media campaigns and by personal experience. Ethical issues are involved in setting 'targets' for health professionals to achieve. Finally, we should remember that even health professionals such as doctors sometimes 'just don't get round to it'.

Chapter 3

Screening and health checks

INTRODUCTION

This chapter will consider the psychological dimensions that are important in identifying who carries out self-examination, most especially breast self-examination, and who presents for health checks and screening. The outcome of such screenings by primary health care teams will be examined. These are areas on which a great deal of recent research has been focused, and it is important to identify what has been learned from these studies.

An aspect of medical services which is at the heart of preventive health is the notion of screening. This process, in theory, enables us to identify potential health problems at an early stage, when, it is hoped, they may be more readily treatable, or their consequences may be more readily dealt with. Screening has become an increasingly important part of the nation's programme to prevent disease and ill health and the process can take many forms. There have been a number of national campaigns to publicise the benefits of screening. Typically, screening takes place in a health setting, but occasionally screening can take place at a person's workplace, school or other establishments. From our point of view there are many aspects of screening that make it an interesting process psychologically. Screening that results in a negative outcome (no disease or pathology found) might be assumed to be reassuring; screening that identifies pathology might be assumed to be potentially anxiety-making. But what about the screening process itself, how much anxiety is generated by the activity of receiving a call for screening, making an appointment, attending, and perhaps most important of all, waiting for a result? Such issues have dominated the psychological research in this area, together with attempts to predict and explain individual differences in uptake or attendance for screening.

WHEN SHOULD WE SCREEN?

Before a screening programme is introduced, several criteria need to be satisfied. Austoker suggests the following general criteria:

- is the condition an important health problem?
- is there a recognisable early stage?
- is treatment at an early stage more beneficial than at a later stage?
- is there a suitable test?
- is the test acceptable to the general population?
- are there adequate facilities for diagnosis and treatment?
- what are the costs and benefits?
- which subgroups should be screened?
- how often should screening take place?

(Austoker, 1994b: 315)

Here are some examples of problems for which screening is currently available: breast cancer, cervical cancer, ovarian cancer, tuberculosis, coronary heart disease, pre-natal abnormalities. It should be apparent fairly rapidly that much screening has been directed at women – breast cancer and cervical cancer are major killers of women, and during pregnancy women will be exposed to the wide range of potential screenings now available for their unborn child. Adult males tend to be involved in fewer screens, coronary heart disease being the most obvious one available. A healthy man of 45 would not expect to be the recipient of any invitations to attend for a preventive health check. A woman of similar age might be offered cervical cancer screening, breast cancer screening and, if she is still using oral contraception, will receive regular blood pressure and weight checks also.

The reasons for this discrepancy between men and women are complex. The best developed areas for screening are those involving the unborn child and hence it is women as child bearers who might be considered here. However, the programmes for cervical and breast cancer are less obviously explicable. It might be argued that these diseases kill large numbers of women, are preventable if detected early enough, and so forth. However, screening for prostate cancer and colectoral cancer, both of which meet these characteristics, is not widely available. Age of onset might also be implicated, but testicular cancer, an increasing killer of young men, is also not well supported by any screening process.

TARGETS FOR SCREENING

With the introduction of GP contracts in 1990, the push to improve screening uptake has gained new momentum. All women aged between 25 and 64 in England should have been invited to receive a cervical smear test during the five years preceding April 1993. If GPs achieve an 80 per cent goal for women in the target group, then they receive full payment to the practice; this drops to one-third potential payment at a 50 per cent achievement, and if the achievement rate falls below 50 per cent then no payment is made at all to the practice. Targets have proved to be very controversial. There has been a clear change in the government's perception of the role and function of the GP in the area of cervical screening. Before 1990 GPs were considered to hold the responsibility for determining the eligibility of women in their practice for the smear test. Since 1990 they have been held responsible for ensuring they achieve the government's definition of eligibility (Singleton and Michael, 1993). In reality, it is nearly always a practice nurse who carries out the smear tests, and the role of the practice nurse has changed and grown in consequence (Cooper *et al.*, 1992). Some GPs have expressed concern about the targets. They fear that women may be 'pressurised' into having a smear test in order that the practice achieves its target:

> A lot of doctors will be very close, if their smear uptake is 79 per cent and they get it up to 80 per cent it could be worth an extra £2,000 per year to them just to get 2 or 3 women to have a smear. Think of the pressure you might put those women under.
>
> (quoted in Singleton and Michael, 1993)

In 1988 the government published recommendations concerning the set up of a computerised system for calling and recalling women for screening. The FHSA (Family Health Services Authority) generates a monthly list of women thought to be due for a smear test. These lists are then sent to GPs who amend the lists according to the known suitability or not of the women for call. Those on the amended list are then sent invitations (often two) to attend for a smear test. Some GPs have expressed concerns about the insensitivity of such procedure to individual patient needs. Inner-city doctors have a rather more mobile population and may, for a number of different reasons, have patients who are less likely to participate in health care services generally (McKie, 1993).

In the United States, the procedures differ somewhat. Since 1990 there have been national and federal attempts to improve screening uptake. A study by Calle *et al.* (1993) examined demographic predictors

of both mammography and pap smear screening. They targeted particularly those whom they defined as under-served groups of women.
They report great variability across basic demographic characteristics.
They found income level to be related to the likelihood of ever having
had a smear test, that Hispanic and Black women were less likely to have
ever had a smear test, and that age was inversely related to ever having
had a smear test. They identify older Black women as being particularly
under-represented in the population achieving a smear test. Never
having been married was an extremely important predictor. As they
report, this is a very difficult finding to interpret in the absence of
information concerning sexual activity, but may have something to do
with the increase in interactions with health professionals that are associated with childbirth and young children.

The direction of almost all research has therefore been to consider
ways in which the target rate of smear tests might be achieved. Very little
research has considered the outcomes of receiving a positive test, and
other dimensions of interest psychologically, with a notable exception to
this being the work of Orbell and Sheeran (1993).

CERVICAL CANCER SCREENING

Screening for cancer of the cervix is one of the longest and best-
established screening programmes available in the UK. Approximately
2000 women a year die from cervical cancer (DoH, 1993). Cervical
cancer is a major cause of death amongst women. Nevertheless, statis-
tically it is still a relatively rare disease. If the disease remains unidentified
until detected at the symptomatic stage, it is usually fatal. Early treatment
of cellular abnormalities can, however, be very effective. Research
indicates that 80 per cent of women dying from cervical cancer have
never had a smear test (Day 1989, cited in McKie, 1993). The aetiology
of the disease is still very poorly understood; incidence of cervical cancer
is positively associated with early age of first intercourse, multiple sexual
partners, cigarette smoking, and possibly a lowered immune system.
Hence the disease is capable of carrying some of the stigma of sexual
activity with its diagnosis. Current policy in the UK is to advocate
screening at least once every five years for women between the ages of
25 and 60 (Scotland) and 20 and 64 (England and Wales). A target has
been set in *The Health of the Nation* for a 20 per cent reduction in the
incidence of cervical cancer by the year 2000 (DOH, 1992a).

Orbell and Sheeran (1993) have carried out a comprehensive survey
of the psychological literature pertaining to cervical cancer screening.

What follows is a summary of their findings. Studies that consider demographic variables show that age is almost always inversely related to uptake of screening (Beardow *et al.*, 1989; Meadows, 1987). There is a lower uptake amongst social classes four and five (Sansom, 1970) and Meadows reports lower uptake in socially stressed areas (Meadows, 1987). Explanations for this variation suggest that chance contact with service providers, and encouragement from GPs are major factors accounting for this difference. Women from lower social classes tend to be in less frequent contact with services and hence have fewer chances for opportunistic encouragement of the service. A study carried out in Oldham, East Lancashire, compared screening uptake of Asian and non-Asian women. Bradley and Friedman (1993) found no difference in uptake between the two groups, but reported that up to 48 per cent of the women in their sample had never received a smear test. Bradley and Friedman also identify missed opportunities when such women might have been approached and encouraged to have a test. A study carried out in a general practice in south London found a negative correlation between the estimated percentage of the practice population from ethnic minority backgrounds and the uptake of the cervical smear test. They also found that uptake rates were significantly higher in practices with a female partner than in those without (Azeem *et al.*, 1994).

Attitudes, beliefs and knowledge of cervical cancer and the cervical screening test are consistently found to be poor (Peters *et al.*, 1989). Not surprisingly, negative attitudes, low knowledge and negative evaluations are found to be more associated with failure to attend for screening. Social influences, whilst hardly researched, seem to indicate that societal pressures, and doctors' encouragement are also important determinants in attending for screening. McKie (1993) reports a small-scale study of seventy non-attenders, of whom she asked what they knew of the causes of cervical cancer. Fifty-seven per cent did not know the causes, and the causes are indeed difficult to identify. Nineteen per cent identified promiscuity as the potential cause and a further 13 per cent identified sexual activity. Finally, 11 per cent suggested other causes such as smoking, the oral contraceptive, a virus and heredity. Clearly there are serious implications from these findings for perceived vulnerability to the disease; most especially, its perceived link with promiscuous sex will affect the likelihood of a women defining herself as potentially 'at risk' of cervical cancer.

Non-attenders for screening have become a particular focus for research study. Orbell and Sheeran collected data from ten studies reported between 1967 and 1989 and they summarise the reasons for non-attendance following an invitation for cervical screening (Orbell and Sheeran, 1993). The highest percentage of reasons for non-attendance concerned other preoccupations at the time – holidays, being just too busy, or an illness are examples given. Nineteen per cent of women indicated a perceived invulnerability to cervical cancer – it is impossible to determine the accuracy of this perception. There are some suggestions that this perceived invulnerability may be related to the 'unrealistic optimism' reported earlier in connection with other health risks. Seventeen per cent cited practical difficulties such as problems with the time or venue for screening. Sixteen per cent reported psychological costs associated with the test procedures (anxiety or embarrassment, for example) and 13 per cent 'forgot'. Thus non-attendance is a combination both of psychological variables and of aspects of how the service is made available to women. It is difficult to interpret the high percentage reporting other preoccupations; this could be influenced by more flexible service provision, but may also mask underlying emotional barriers to the screening procedures. A recent study by McKie (1993) asked non-attenders if there was anything that might trigger them to request a smear test. Women cited the presence of symptoms as a potential trigger most frequently (37 per cent), and social pressure, predominantly from family or friends, as the only other possible trigger (17 per cent). Since the presence of symptoms is an indication of serious, if not fatal, progression of the disease, this finding is particularly concerning.

Three models of health behaviours have been applied to cervical cancer screening. Inevitably, the Health Belief Model has generated much research. Hennig and Knowles (1990) and Hill *et al.* (1985) both report that intention to attend is significantly related to perceived vulnerability to cervical cancer and non-attendance is linked to perceived barriers to attendance. In both studies the amount of variance accounted for was low, as we have come to expect (32 per cent and 27 per cent respectively). The same researchers have also considered the Theory of Reasoned Action and once again found significant, but extremely modest, support for the model. Orbell and Sheeran (1993) argue convincingly that models that combine psychological variables with a consideration of aspects of service provision and delivery stand the best chance of predicting and explaining the uptake of cervical screening opportunities.

OVARIAN CANCER

Ovarian cancer is the fifth most common cancer in women. In 1992, 4,360 women died from ovarian cancer; most cases occur in women over the age of 45 and most women present with an advanced stage of the disease. The overall survival rate is about 28 per cent. Early detection can improve this rate of survival, hence ovarian cancer would seem to be a good candidate for screening. However, there are limitations to the usefulness of screening. Because the overall incidence of ovarian cancer in the female population is low, 5,000 women would have to be screened for one case of the cancer to be diagnosed. Furthermore, fifty women from this group would have a false positive result. Two screening procedures have been developed and they show promise; but at the moment, Austoker (1994) concludes that screening for ovarian cancer should not be offered routinely to asymptomatic women.

GENERAL HEALTH CHECKS

Other researchers have studied factors that might be important in the uptake of general health checks offered by GPs via Well Persons Clinics (Norman 1993, Norman and Fitter, 1991). Usually these checks involve a visit to the surgery and an interview with a practice nurse. A patient's body mass index, blood pressure, cholesterol, smoking, drinking and exercise levels are recorded and health promotion advice is dispensed. Norman found significant differences in attendance rates according to the way in which patients were invited. He suggests that an invitation letter can be just as effective as opportunistic invitations, with the bonus that it is an easier method to implement and monitor. However, either method achieved only around 62 per cent uptake. The Health Belief Model proved wholly inadequate in predicting uptake; health value (how much a person values good health) was the best predictor of attendance, but accounted for only 4 per cent of attendance behaviour in a multiple regression analysis.

It is not wholly clear how beneficial these generalised health checks are and how far patients adhere to the advice being given. My own observation is that being given an 'all clear' is sometimes interpreted as receiving the go ahead to indulge oneself in which ever vices invite – cream cakes, white wine, whatever. I can find no research that seriously considers the possibility that such 'boomerang' behaviour might result, but there is some small amount of evidence (Tymstra and Bielmen, 1987 and Kinlay and Heller, 1990, cited by Marteau, 1993) that reports an inappropriately high level of reassurance following a negative result from a genetic antenatal screening procedure.

CORONARY HEART DISEASE

Similar in style to the general checks discussed above are the attempts to reduce the rate of heart disease via preventive checks and advice. Two large-scale studies involving around 18,000 people have recently reported some fairly pessimistic outcomes to these attempts. The British Family Heart Study (Wood *et al.*, 1994) concluded that government initiatives in these directions were misguided: 'We believe the results of this study . . . justify a change in Government policy in relation to voluntary health promotion packages in general practice' (*Guardian* 28/1/94). They conclude there is no good evidence that such strategies result in reduction either in levels of cholesterol, or in achieving changes in eating, drinking or exercise patterns.

The second study, known as OXCHECK, advocated the retargeting of resources at those who were known to be at high risk, such as middle-aged men with angina, high blood pressure and those who had already had small strokes and heart attacks. Thus there already seems to be a move away from mass screening toward checks that are more focused or targeted. It has yet to be seen whether these preliminary findings are confirmed when the studies are completed, and, if so, whether the government will rethink this national strategy.

Coronary heart disease has a number of risk factors: being male, being a smoker, having high blood pressure, and others. Risk factors interrelate and interact such that the relative risk of dying from CHD for a smoker with high blood pressure is about four times greater than non-smokers with low blood pressure, taking blood cholesterol as similar in both groups (Rose, 1992).

Blood cholesterol is considered to be an important risk factor for coronary heart disease. Cholesterol is a natural fat or lipid that is manufactured in the body. Variations in cholesterol are associated with mortality from coronary heart disease. The relationship between blood cholesterol and risk is a continuous one. Variations in blood cholesterol across communities are usually associated with dietary factors. A community with a high dietary fat intake and a low ratio of polyunsaturated to saturated fatty acids tends to higher blood cholesterol levels. What this means on an individual level, however, is less clear.

In spite of these complexities, there have been calls to introduce mass screening for blood cholesterol. Those people identified above a specified cut off point would be considered for treatment programmes, either diet modification or drug based, to lower their levels of cholesterol. The large-scale Framingham study in the United States showed a great overlap in the blood cholesterol levels of the men in their sample between those who subsequently developed heart disease and those who did not. Thus a simple measure of blood cholesterol level as a means of identifying individuals at risk of CHD would wrongly target a number of healthy men who would *not* later become sick through CHD. The consequences of this mis-targeting in terms of increased unnecessary anxiety might well be detrimental to their health. Much more positive outcomes can be achieved by targeting screening at individuals independently identified as at 'high risk' for CHD. In the UK recently this has been estimated to be around 2 per cent of middle-aged men. For such a small proportion to benefit there is a high cost to initiate a national screening programme for blood cholesterol. It would be more appropriate at this stage to identify ways in which general practitioners and others can readily and easily identify these 'high risk' men. These concerns were captured in 1989 by Smith *et al.* in the following elegant quotation:

> Screening programmes in which doctors approach apparently healthy individuals to make them patients for a lifetime, ethically must ensure that treatment . . . does more good than harm.

COLORECTAL AND PROSTATE CANCER

Prostate cancer is the second most common cancer among men in the United Kingdom. The incidence of the cancer is increasing, partly because of increased longevity, since nearly all cancers of the colon and prostate occur in people over the age of 50. Deaths from prostate cancer peak between the ages of 75 and 79. Some increase in the rate of these cancers may also be the result of changes in lifestyle and diet. The five-year survival rate for cancer of the prostate is 43 per cent, largely because of the late stage of presentation. In the United States there have been a number of screening initiatives for these cancers; screening is often carried out via a digital rectal examination, but the method has only limited sensitivity. Enthusiasm for routine screening for these cancers has been limited in the UK; a recent study declared routine screening for prostate cancer in men over 50 a waste of resources. The study calculated that screening increases life expectancy by between 0.6 and 1.7 days only. They also argue that the stigma associated with a diagnosis for cancer and the treatment of the disease could lead to a decline in the quality of life; hence one might conclude that screening would be of more harm than good. Austoker (1994b) summarises the case against routine screening for cancer of the prostate by estimating that only a few years of life would be saved and that the reduction in overall mortality from screening would be very limited.

BREAST CANCER

Screening for breast cancer has probably been more fully researched than any other screening programme. Breast cancer is the leading cause of cancer-related deaths among women. Approximately one in twelve women in the UK will develop breast cancer during her life time and more than 15,000 women die from it each year. The United Kingdom has the highest standardised mortality rate of breast cancer in the world; it is not surprising, therefore, that it should be the focus of much research. Other factors make the investigation of psychological dimensions of this disease an important focus of study. If breast cancer can be detected at an early stage, the prognosis is very much better. Ninety-one per cent of women with breast cancer discovered at Stage One will be alive in five years' time as opposed to 18 per cent of those who have tumours advanced to Stage Four. Various strategies for prevention of breast cancer are possible. From the point of view of this chapter, mammography and breast self-examination are important strategies.

Mammography is increasingly available in the UK for women between the ages of 50 and 64. The setting of these age limits is in itself controversial. The argument for not extending the limit downwards to, say, 40 concerns the cost effectiveness of the screening programme. It also relies on evidence from the USA and Sweden that screening over the age of 50 is effective in reducing mortality (Shapiro *et al.*, 1985). The same study and others (Taber *et al.* 1985, 1989) also found no significant reduction in mortality by offering women between 40 and 50 mammography. The fact is that a large number of women between the ages of 35 and 50 contract breast cancer each year in this country. For them the screening programme is too late. The upper age limit is possibly even harder to justify. Breast cancer deaths in women above the age of 65 are not less common and yet such women are not routinely called for screening. Once again the arguments tend to centre around the loss to the country of a 'productive' member of the community, and the unstated acknowledgement that people over retirement age are due to die sooner rather than later. In an era of scarce resources it is not surprising that such hard economic decisions are made; what is important is that the under-lying bases for these decisions are at least clarified, and discussed, if not challenged, fairly frequently. A major review article by White *et al.* (1993) considers the cost effectiveness of mammography in the United States. They conclude that the estimated cost of annual mammography relative to clinical breast examination is $36,000 per year of life saved (about £23,000 by current exchange rates). They remind readers that 'the criterion of cost effectiveness is that the strategy must yield a benefit worth its cost' (White *et al.*, 1993: 630) and they argue that a very careful consideration of the cost effectiveness of breast cancer screening is required.

Targets for mammography programmes are therefore set within the age bands outlined. A UK trial screening programme reported in 1988 showed that 69 per cent of women invited for an initial screen in southern England responded, and 63 per cent in Scotland. Vaile *et al.* (1993) examined the demographic characteristics of attenders and found that such factors played little part in attendance. The only exception was the finding that married women were more likely to attend than those who were single, widowed, separated or divorced. This finding is hard to explain. The role of 'significant others' in encouraging women to seek screening might be important here, but also it is possible that unmarried women of this age are more likely to be in full-time employment and hence might find attendance at the clinic difficult to arrange. We saw a similar pattern emerging earlier in the chapter for screening for cervical cancer.

Amongst those who did attend a screening, Vaile *et al.* identify two major sources of dissatisfaction that might impede future attendance. The first is the delay in notification of results. The second is the finding that a significant proportion of women reported discomfort and pain from the procedures. A mammographic screening is frequently described as pain-less in promotional literature, yet 40 per cent of Vaile's sample of over 3,000 women reported discomfort and up to 20 per cent reported pain. This finding is to be the subject of further study and is clearly an important dimension of the screening initiative which seems to have been hardly addressed so far.

Finally, a significant proportion of women who attend for screening will be recalled for further investigation (usually around 10 per cent). Two or three of these women may undergo a biopsy, and one will be found to have cancer. These 'false positives' have not been extensively researched, and yet it is not difficult to imagine the psychological impact of a recall or follow-up such as this.

A study by Rakowski *et al.* (1992) examines women's decisions about mammography from the transtheoretical model of behaviour change (Prochaska and DiClemente, 1982). The model proposes a sequence of stages along a continuum of behavioural change. The first stage, known as precontemplation, assumes no intention of adopting the target behaviour; the second stage, contemplation, involves considering adoption of the new behaviour; the third action involves initiating the new behaviour and the fourth, maintenance, concerns sustaining the adopted behaviour over a period of time. Each stage involves decision-making and the progression is not necessary linear, that is, the model tries to allow for the possibility of relapse to an earlier stage. Translated for mammography, Rakowski *et al.* describe the stages of adoption as follows:

1 Precontemplation: no prior mammogram and no plan for one in the coming year
2 Contemplation: either, no prior mammogram but a plan for one in the coming year; or, one or more prior mammograms but no plan for one in the coming year
3 Action: one prior mammogram and planning for one in the coming year
4 Maintenance: more than one prior mammogram and planning for one in the coming year.

(Rakowski *et al.*, 1992: 112)

Rakowski's findings support an analysis of intention to attend for mammography via the transtheoretical model. This is particularly interesting since much early work with this model focused on the avoidance of a potentially harmful activity, i.e. contemplating giving up smoking, or cutting down on fat intake, rather than on the uptake of a potentially healthy activity such as seeking screening. In a burst of enthusiasm, Rakowski *et al.* suggest that the model might be extended to other screening and early detection procedures: 'Sigmoidoscopy, stool testing, cholesterol testing, prostate examinations and glaucoma testing are all amenable to the strategies used in our study' (1992: 117). Other researchers have used other models to examine mammography. Jepsom and Rimer (1993) report a study of determinants of mammography intentions and behaviours using both the Health Belief Model and the Theory of Reasoned Action. They found substantial differences between women who had had a prior screening and women who had not. They found many significant differences between the two groups of women. They also claim

Our findings for nonscreenees might be said to represent a triumph of the accumulated wisdom of past research and theory on health related decision making. Out of a set of nineteen variables representing standard demographic factor and central concepts from theoretical formulations (HBM and TRA), nine contributed significantly to a multivariate model of mammography intentions, predicting nearly half of the variance in intention scores.

(Jepson and Rimer, 1993: 48)

The results for women who had previously attended for a screening were less impressive; only around one-sixth of the total variance associated with intention was accounted for. Even with this outcome, we should remember that it is not a behaviour that we are successfully predicting here, only the intention to perform a behaviour. We have still a very long way to go in our attempts to predict and understand why some women 'comply' with an invitation to attend a mammography screening, while others do not.

SELF-EXAMINATION

Given the costs of screening outlined above, and the difficulties in persuading people to attend such screening programmes, it is important to consider other activities related to the early detection of disease. A preventive health behaviour that has attracted much psychological interest and research is the practice of self-examination. This can be defined as the practice of examining one's body in a systematic fashion for the purpose of detecting an abnormality. Self-examination is simple, completely safe, and economical; the questions concern whether it works as a means of detecting abnormalities at an early stage of development and whether the practice itself carries any psychological risks, such as, for example, an increase in anxiety. Breast self-examination (BSE) is claimed to be effective in promoting the detection of breast tumours at an early clinical stage and of small size (Foster *et al.*, 1978; Champion and Scott, 1993). Considering the potential advantages of regular BSE it is perhaps surprising that relatively few women practise it. Frequency reports suggest that as few as 19 per cent of American women practise BSE regularly (Craun and Deffenbacher, 1987); other studies report even lower levels, such as 11 per cent (McCaul *et al.*, 1993). Studies in Britain have found similar levels for BSE (Nichols, 1983; Owens *et al.*, 1987). Psychologists have sought to explain the problems associated with developing and adhering to a health related behaviour such as this via social cognition models. Many studies have considered BSE from the point of view of the Health Belief Model (Champion, 1994; Champion and Scott, 1993). It is interesting to note though that the relationship between BSE and breast cancer is complex. Self-examination does not reduce the chances of contracting breast cancer, and to practise BSE actually increases the likelihood of finding a lump and hence the possibility of identifying cancer. Thus the perceived benefits of BSE need to be qualified. Lowering a woman's susceptibility to breast cancer is not a feasible goal (benefit), but lessening the consequences of the disease may be.

Specific benefits that have been found to correlate positively with BSE are: a belief that if or when a lump is found something can be done, a belief in the advantages of BSE and a belief that a positive attitude towards BSE is possible. Barriers to BSE have been found to be the woman's confidence level (Edwards, 1980), lack of knowledge concerning detection levels and the ability to detect a lump (McCusker and Morrow, 1977), and lack of privacy to practise the behaviour (Zapka and Mamon, 1982).

A number of scales of perceived benefits/barriers and susceptibility to breast cancer have been developed, for example by Stillman (1977). Significant associations between BSE practice and the scale have been reported by Stillman (1977) and Hallal (1982). Stillman reported 87 per cent of her sample of 122 women scored highly for perceived susceptibility – far higher than the 9–12 per cent who will actually contract breast cancer. Ninety-seven per cent thought BSE was beneficial, yet only 40 per cent practised BSE monthly. Rutledge (1987) studied 93 volunteer women. She again found perceived benefits/barriers to be directly related to BSE. She did not, however, find a relationship between perceived susceptibility and frequency of practice of BSE, which is probably explained by the fact that BSE does not reduce *susceptibility* to breast cancer per se. Calnan and his colleagues have also examined the Health Belief Model and BSE (Calnan, 1984). He found that the variables that contribute to the Health Belief Model were amongst the best predictors of attendance at a class teaching BSE and at a clinic offering mammography, but that the amount of variance explained by these variables was small. Self-concept and self-esteem are factors that have been shown also to influence the likelihood of BSE (Hallal, 1982; Rutledge, 1987).

McCaul *et al.* (1993) considered BSE via the Theory of Reasoned Action. They found that attitudes and subjective norms predicted intentions to perform BSE (R squared 0.34). Fletcher *et al.* (1989) examined the relationship between women's sociodemographic characteristics, knowledge, attitudes and beliefs to BSE. They found the most important single predictor of BSE was type of employment, accounting for approximately 9 per cent of the variance, with a general interest in health matters accounting for a further 5 per cent. Studies such as these indicate that a search for single predictors of such practices as BSE are not likely to result in findings that can meaningfully be incorporated into educational programmes. This last finding also reminds us how important social and demographic, as well as psychological, variables are in our search for predictors of behaviour. There has regularly been reported a negative association between age and the practice of preventive health behaviours, e.g. Gould-Martin *et al.*, 1982, and others. This finding has particular importance for BSE as the older a woman is, the more likely she is to develop a breast lump.

Hobbs *et al.* (1984) review the evidence that teaching programmes on BSE can influence the opinions and knowledge of women about the advantages of early detection and treatment. They argue though that such changes in knowledge have little direct effect on the extent to which BSE is actually practised. It seems from the women's comments that the difficulties lie in knowing exactly what to do, and when and how often to do it. It is also the case that women are not particularly well informed about the risk factors associated with breast cancer; they are by and large unable to make a realistic assessment of their own susceptibility to the disease and tend to over-estimate the personal risks. Such over-estimation may result in fear and denial as coping strategies. Further information that seeks both to reassure and educate women as to the actual incidence of breast cancer and the relative frequency of benign lumps, linked with detailed information on the practice of BSE, could further reduce the number of women failing to carry out this procedure.

Few attempts have been made to introduce self-examination practices in less-developed countries; given their cost effectiveness, this is strange. A study in Monterey (Sheley and Lesan, 1986) suggested that general campaigns were unlikely to be effective; campaigns needed to be targeted specifically at women likely to benefit from such messages. A similar study in Zimbabwe sought to identify the prerequisites necessary for the introduction of such a campaign. Pitts *et al.* (1994) suggested that Zimbabwean women needed basic information about the incidence of breast cancer, the risk factors associated with the disease, the mechanisms of self-examination, and the fact that most palpable lumps are non-malignant.

TESTICULAR CANCER

The lessons learned from a consideration of the processes that influence the practice of BSE can be extended to other cancers. For example, testicular cancer can be cured if treated early and similar techniques of self-examination can be taught to men, or their partners, to enable abnormalities to be detected before they are at an advanced stage. Testicular cancer is the commonest cancer for men aged 20–34. More than half the cases of testicular cancer occur in men under the age of 35. Testicular cancer is highly susceptible to modern treatment with a survival rate of nearly 100 per cent if the cancer is detected early. The major risk factor for testicular cancer is cryptorchism (undescended testis). There is an increased risk of three to four fold with one undescended testicle and a ten fold increase in risk for two undescended testes. McCaul *et al.* (1993) found support for the theory of planned behaviour as a moderate predictor of intentions to perform testicular self-examination (TSE) in a student sample. They also found self-efficacy to have an additional, but weak role (McCaul *et al.*, 1993; Brubaker and Fowler, 1990; Brubaker and Wickersham, 1990). These studies, unfortunately, did not examine the actual behaviour of self-examination, but only the stated intention to perform it. Neef *et al.* (1991) questioned college students in the US. They found that more than 41 per cent had been taught TSE, 22 per cent had examined their testicles at least once, but only 8 per cent reported practising TSE once a month. A comparative study of British and Zimbabwean undergraduates also reported extremely low levels in both countries (Pitts *et al.*, 1994).

MELANOMA AND SELF-EXAMINATION

Skin cancers are associated with many of the characteristics that make screening or self-examination programmes a good option. McCarthy and Shaw (1989) report that a cure rate of 100 per cent for some skin cancers can be achieved if lesions are detected early enough.

Education about melanomas can lead to the seeking of medical advice at an early stage of skin cancer. Screening can either be achieved via self-examination, or via examination by another person, often a health professional. Hennrikus *et al.* (1991) reported delay in seeking medical advice following detection of abnormalities associated with skin cancer. Reasons for such delays were usually the result of a lack of sufficient information about the significance of signs of possible skin cancer. Almost half the people surveyed by Hennrikus thought the signs were not serious, and an additional 27 per cent employed a 'wait and see' strategy. Eiser *et al.* (1993) have carried out one of the few studies based in the UK. They interviewed an opportunistic sample of 176 university students and report some interesting gender differences. Previous studies had found that men took fewer precautions against skin cancer than women (Cody and Lee, 1990) even though they were more likely to be exposed to the sun during their working day. Women in Eiser's study were more prepared to protect themselves appropriately, most especially by the use of sunscreens, but also tended to value sun-bathing more highly than men. Thus their greater approval of protection may be based on greater need. However, it is clear that a focus for future research should be amongst men who are exposed to the sun via their work rather than via their leisure since this group seems to be less well researched, and much less aware of the risks they run.

PRENATAL SCREENING

Prenatal screening is now a routine part of the experience of pregnancy for most women in the western world. There are clear and obvious benefits of the screening process, but there are also potential costs associated with increased anxiety and its effects on both mother and her baby. Theresa Marteau, with others, has carried out extensive research on the psychological concomitants of prenatal screening. Marteau reports that mothers often do not know *why* they are being screened. She reports that 39 per cent of women undergoing a blood test for spina bifida were unaware of the disorder for which they were being screened. (Marteau *et al.*, 1988). Marteau suggests that many health professionals believe that providing too much information to women will needlessly increase their level of anxiety. Her study in 1993 examined whether provision of detailed information about prenatal screening increased patients' knowledge and satisfaction and decreased their anxiety. Women were randomly allocated to one of five groups. Group one received a booklet about the alpha-fetaprotein test; group two was offered an antenatal class; group three was offered both options, and groups four and five were controls. The study offered partial support for her hypotheses in that the provision of detailed information was associated with an increase in knowledge and satisfaction, but there was no clear link with anxiety, most particularly for those women who received an abnormal alpha-fetaprotein test result. This latter finding is extremely surprising and goes against earlier work by Marteau and others which, not surprisingly, reports increased anxiety associated with an abnormal test result (Marteau *et al.*, 1988, 1992).

Concerns have been expressed at the 'over-extensive' use of scans. The *Observer* carried a report on a public enquiry held in South Wales which heard evidence from several women who were told that their babies were dead when a scan showed no foetal heart beat. Some had to wait for up to ten days to receive confirmation that their babies were in fact still alive. A consultant is quoted as saying 'a bad scan is worse than no scan'.

Genetic screening is inevitably an extremely controversial issue. A recent example of a screening programme aimed at a specific target report is reported in the *Observer*, March 1994. Tay Sachs disease has an incidence amongst Ashkenazi Jews one hundred times higher than in any other group. The gene is recessive, which means that both parents need to be carriers for a child to be born with Tay Sachs. Arranged marriages are also customary amongst orthodox Jews; hence the opportunity exists to avoid relationships where both parties are carriers. In New York there is a screening programme for Tay Sachs that can be used by partners intending to marry; this programme is now being extended to consider cystic fibrosis and Gaucher's disease, both diseases where the outcomes are less predictable. One can see the beginning of concerns here, illustrated by a comment: 'I don't know where this stops, or who makes the decision where this stops' (*Observer*, March 1994).

HEALTH PROFESSIONAL FACTORS

Marteau and Johnston (1990) have argued for the increasing need to consider the health-related beliefs and behaviours of the health professionals who are providing advice and care to patients. Woo *et al.* (1985) found that doctors with a family history of cancer were significantly more likely to recommend cancer screening than those with no history. Health professionals' knowledge of disease and the role of screening will also affect patients' responses (Marteau, 1993).

GETTING THE RESULTS OF SCREENING

Marteau (1993) reviews the evidence of the impact of undergoing screening. The time between attending for screening and receiving the result is inevitably an anxious one. I referred earlier to the work on prenatal screening. Reactions to breast screening have also been studied. Fallowfield *et al.* (1990) carried out a retrospective study of women who had attended for breast screening. Ninety-three per cent reported that they were pleased they had received an invitation, but 55 per cent also reported feeling worried. Nathoo (1988) traced women who had not attended for cervical screening and reported that twelve out of seventeen reported terror; some had the assumption that their doctor had reason to suppose they *had* cervical cancer and that was why they had been called for screening. Increased public awareness of the nature of routine screening will presumably help to alleviate some of these problems.

CONCLUSION

This has been a fairly brief excursion into a major area of health research and one that lies at the heart of preventive health care. Psychologists have already contributed a great deal to the understanding of the public's responses to screening and self-examination. Decisions concerning whom to screen and for what are, of course, critical, and those decisions are the province of government and health policy advisers. Psychologists might usefully study those decision-making processes also.

Chapter 4

Lifestyle research

Health promotion places responsibility for much illness and disease in the western world upon lifestyle behaviours. This chapter will consider the evidence for the effects of drinking, smoking and exercise on an individual's health. It will also examine the effectiveness of some of the attempts to modify these behaviours.

DRINKING

Drinking alcohol provides pleasure and comfort to many people. It is part of many cultures and associated with significant rituals and life events – a birth, a marriage, a promotion, success in an examination; many of these occasions have alcohol as a key feature of the social event. However, the other side of alcohol – its negative effects on health, wealth and relationships – is also extremely well known. Heavy alcohol use is associated with increased morbidity and mortality. Health consequences of heavy use of alcohol include liver damage, cardiovascular and intestinal diseases and accidents. A recent estimate suggested that around 28,000 deaths each year in England and Wales are associated with alcohol consumption (Anderson, 1988). More than 3,000 deaths each year are the result of chronic liver disease and other consequences of alcohol poisoning (DoH, 1993). Other less well-known associations with alcohol are increased risk for cancers of the pharynx and larynx (Anderson *et al.*, 1993) and a fairly large increase in risk to women of breast cancer (Longnecker and MacMahon, 1988).

As a general rule, there is a direct relationship between the amount of alcohol consumed and the degree of increased risk: the more you drink the more likely you are to suffer from drink-related illness. There is though the exception of teetotallers. Non-drinkers are typically found to have higher mortality than light drinkers. The reasons for this are extremely complex to

...e. Non-drinkers are unlikely to be a homogenous group who ...particular characteristics; some may not be drinking for religious ...sons, hence cultural and ethnic differences may be important, others may not be drinking because of existing health problems or regular use of medication where drinking is a contra-indicator, hence they may already be at increased risk of mortality and morbidity because of the predisposing illness. Who knows whom the others are?

The evidence in favour of the health advantages of light drinking, however, is easier to evaluate. A number of studies (Marmot and Bruner, 1991; Shaper, 1990; Eadie, 1991) show that two units of alcohol a day may improve cardiovascular functioning in men, and hence protect against coronary heart disease. There has been further work that has attempted to go beyond 'units of alcohol' and identify benefits associated with particular drinks, most especially red wine. For those of us who are fond of wine of any hue this is welcome as a reason (if not excuse) for some fairly regular light consumption. However, the evidence is very limited in what it can tell us; for example, women are severely under-represented in the research, and other beverages are under-researched. The whisky prescribed by the family doctor last thing at night as an aid to sleep may have more than psychological benefits, but we cannot yet be sure.

Enough of the benefits of alcohol. They are overwhelmed by the evidence of the seriousness of heavy drinking. *The Health of the Nation* (DoH, 1992a) has set targets to reduce the proportion of men consuming more than 21 units per week from 28 per cent to 18 per cent and for women from 11 per cent to 7 per cent by the year 2005. A unit of alcohol is approximately one glass of wine, a measure of spirits, or a half pint of standard beer or lager. The government has just raised these advisory limits to 21 units per week for women and 28 for men (December 1995). Drinkers of more than these limits per week are identified as 'hazardous' in that they consume sufficient alcohol to put themselves at greater risk of ill health than those consuming within government limits. If they are already experiencing problems as a result of alcohol consumption such people would be known as 'harmful' drinkers. Around 9 per cent of women are drinking between 15 and 35 units of alcohol per week, and 2 per cent are drinking above this limit. The equivalent statistics for men show the possibility of a much greater incidence of 'problem drinking': 73 per cent stay within the recommended limit of 21 units or less per week, 20 per cent are drinking between 22 and 50 units and 7 per cent are consuming more than 50 units per week. That is, men in this last group are drinking more than 25 pints of beer, around ten bottles of wine or nearly two bottles of whisky per week as a minimum.

Alcohol consumption is highest amongst young adults and increases with income. Certain occupations are associated with high levels of drinking; these are best characterised as those where alcohol is readily available (publicans, for example) and those where high levels of stress occur. It might be, of course, that people may be attracted to certain occupations because of the availability of alcohol, but this is unlikely to account for the fact that publicans, bar staff and others in the catering trade, members of the forces, airline pilots and ships officers are between three and ten times more likely to die from cirrhosis of the liver against the standardised mortality rate. Doctors, clergy, lawyers and journalists also have a somewhat increased risk. The most striking increase in drinking has occurred amongst women. Twenty years ago deaths from alcoholic cirrhosis were five times as common in men as in women; now that ratio is 1.5:1 (Paton, 1994).

Ledermann, a French mathematician, developed a hypothesis that the average intake of alcohol by a population can predict the prevalence of heavy drinking. He suggests alcohol consumption is normally distributed in a population; that there is no clear division between 'alcoholics' and 'normal drinkers'; and that around 10 per cent of the population consume half the total amount of alcohol drunk (Ledermann, 1964, 1965). His work has been heavily criticised on methodological grounds but Rose (1992) supports the underlying reasoning that it is possible to predict the number of heavy drinkers from knowing the average alcohol intake of the population, and that changes in the average consumption of alcohol in a population will also change the prevalence of heavy drinking and equivalent health-related problems.

Paton (1994) estimates the costs to society of alcohol misuse. He quotes estimates of a loss to industry of £770 million and 14 million days through sickness absence. Obviously, one must also remember the revenue to government, which has been estimated at at least £7 billion (or £13,000 per minute) and the quarter of a million people employed in the drinks industry.

Political action to control harmful drinking has, in certain aspects, been impressive, but by no means in all. Price seems to be an effective regulator of alcohol consumption, as does availability. The latter is increasing in the UK with the widespread sales of alcohol via super-market outlets and the increased pub opening hours. However, there has been no obvious increase in consumption since the licensing laws were liberalised in 1989 in England and Wales. Other countries have clearly differing levels of harmful drinking, and this can be shown to be directly related to availability. Cirrhosis mortality in France is the highest in the world at around ten times that of the UK. The Occupation during the Second World War reduced the availability of alcohol significantly; within two years the death rate had dropped, almost to the UK level. Following the end of the Occupation it rose again, and within five years had returned to its prewar level (Rose, 1992). Cirrhosis of the liver takes many years to develop; a last bout of heavy drinking is, though, what is most likely to finish someone off and that is what Rose's analysis claims to show in war-time France.

Advertising by the drinks industry is widespread and costs around £300 million a year; set against this, the budget of the Health Education Authority of £4 million to inform us of the health risks of drinking excessively is fairly unimpressive. The policy in the United States is much tougher than the UK. A Federal Law in 1984 withdrew funds from states that permitted the sale of alcohol to anyone under the age of 21 years; such a debate has yet even to begin in the UK.

One area where public campaigns do seem to have had a decided effect is in drink-driving. Campaigns at Christmas have resulted in reductions year upon year of the number of people prosecuted for being over the limit. Breathalysers and the severe consequences of a drink-driving conviction have played a part in the reduction of alcohol-related car accidents.

MEASURING ALCOHOL CONSUMPTION

The most accurate ways to measure alcohol consumption are, of course, via blood or urine sampling – the kinds of measures that would have some status in a court of law. Psychologists, working outside a laboratory setting, have great difficulty using such measures, and clearly their role in health promotion would be extremely problematic. Instead, there have been developed a number of simple screening questionnaires that have been widely validated as accurate measures of alcohol consumption. They do, of course, carry with them the problems associated with any self-reports, particularly for behaviours that potentially could carry with them the stigma of 'alcoholism'. Comparisons across different screening instruments are difficult since they have often been devised and validated in different settings. Many of the early instruments were designed to detect alcoholism, and not to screen for problem drinking at an earlier stage. An example would be MAST, the Michigan Alcoholism Screening Test, which has been widely used and frequently modified. The MAST correctly identified 98 per cent of alcoholics and falsely identified only 5 per cent of non-alcoholics.

Another widely used measure is CAGE. CAGE asks four questions covering:

- Cut Down – have you ever thought you should cut down on your drinking?
- Annoyed – have you ever been annoyed by other people's criticisms of your drinking?
- Guilt – have you ever felt guilty about your drinking and
- Early Morning drink – have you ever had an early morning drink to steady your nerves (an eye opener)?

These four questions are used as a scale where two or more positive responses are regarded as evidence for potentially hazardous drinking levels.

AUDIT has been developed via the World Health Organisation and is also designed to detect harmful or hazardous drinking. It specifically focuses on detecting drinkers before they 'qualify' for the alcoholic label. AUDIT stands for the Alcohol Use Disorders Identification Test. It has been developed and tested in a number of different situations and in a number of different countries and as such is potentially an extremely useful measure to allow comparisons to be made across different groups. It has ten items, covering alcohol consumption, 'How often do you have a drink containing alcohol?', and symptoms and consequences of alcohol use, 'How often have you been unable to remember what happened the night before because you have been drinking?'. Scoring has a minimum of 0 – for non-drinkers – up to a maximum possible score of 40. A score of 8 of more is taken as indicating a strong likelihood of hazardous or harmful alcohol consumption (Sanders *et al.*, 1993). It has high sensitivity in that it can detect 92 per cent of harmful or hazardous drinkers, and good specificity (it can correctly identify 94 per cent of people drinking below the recommended levels). The differences between AUDIT and other measures are that it seeks to detect problems at the less severe end of the spectrum, it places considerable emphasis on hazardous consumption and frequency of intoxication, and because it does not involve a yes/no format, it relies less on the respondent identifying him or herself as a problem drinker.

Such measures can be used to some considerable effect in the primary health care setting. The kinds of screening devices described above could be fruitfully used during routine consultations with GPs. A study by Wallace *et al.* in 1988 found that the use of a screening device in a single practice increased the identification of people with alcohol-related problems by 80 per cent. However, some GPs seem unwilling to develop work in this area, and a recent survey of 5,000 adults found that only 2 per cent reported any discussion related to alcohol use with any health professional in the past year (Health Education Authority). The screens have been used more widely in hospitals, where opportunistic screening has identified very high levels of harmful or hazardous drinkers. A number of studies have estimated that around 20 per cent of adult admissions to general hospital may be in the harmful or hazardous group.

REDUCING HAZARDOUS ALCOHOL CONSUMPTION

There have been a number of studies that have examined the effectiveness of a brief intervention in reducing alcohol consumption. A study by the World Health Organisation in 1992 considered results from eight centres around the world where, in a randomised controlled trial, they examined patients who reported drinking on average more than 44 units per week (men) or more than 28 units per week (women). A control group who simply received the assessment were compared with intervention groups who received either assessment and advice about the harmful effects of their drinking together with a booklet of information, or who received assessment, advice and four brief counselling sessions and a manual.

Intervention was found to be effective over controls in five of the eight centres (Australia, UK, USA, USSR and Zimbabwe) for male drinkers. These drinkers reduced their alcohol consumption by nearly 25 per cent when compared with the controls. For women, the effect was less dramatic with a 10 per cent reduction for the intervention group over the control group. However, all groups of women (including the controls) reduced their consumption considerably following the assessment. No difference was found between the two kinds of intervention, with no apparent additional benefits accruing from the counselling sessions. This is powerful evidence for the role of information provision in reducing harmful drinking. It also suggests that self-monitoring of alcohol consumption may be effective in itself in reducing it, most especially for women.

Another well-controlled study was that reported by Wallace *et al.* in 1988. People were identified via general practices in England and Scotland using CAGE and included in the trials if they consumed more than 35 units per week (men) and more than 20 units per week (women). Those randomised to the control group received no information concerning their alcohol consumption; patients in the treatment group were contacted by their GP and invited to attend for interview. Rather more than 60 per cent did attend and at interview were advised of the potential harmful effects of their drinking and given an information booklet. Follow-up interviews were offered and at the end of one year patients were assessed by an independent rater as to their current level of alcohol consumption. There was a 21 per cent reduction in alcohol consumption among men in the intervention group when compared with the controls; a slightly larger response was found in women. Self-report was also compared with biological markers to check the reliability of the self-report and support for the self reports was found.

A complex design was employed by Harris and Miller (1990) to address the issue of whether initial assessment of drinking levels was the main factor in producing change in drinking patterns. Following an initial assessment, they randomised problem drinkers into a minimal intervention group, an outpatient counselling group, or into one of two control groups. The first control group was instructed simply to wait ten weeks for treatment; the other control group kept a self-monitoring diary of drinking habits over a ten-week period. Both intervention groups showed a significant change in drinking behaviour over the ten-week period, reducing consumption by two-thirds, and neither intervention group did significantly better than the other. There were no equivalent changes in the two control groups, which showed that self-monitoring by itself is not sufficient to achieve change in drinking patterns.

Bien et al. (1993) summarise the common elements of effective brief interventions from their review of 32 controlled studies. They itemise six elements, taken from Miller and Sanchez (1993), which together seem to constitute an effective intervention. As seems to be the norm in this area of research, they characterise the elements by an acronym: FRAMES. This stands for:

- FEEDBACK of personal risk or impairment, emphasis on personal
- RESPONSIBILITY for change,
- clear ADVICE to change,
- a MENU of alternative change options,
- therapeutic EMPATHY as a counselling style, and finally,
- enhancement of client SELF-EFFICACY or optimism.

An intervention that contains these key elements is considered the most likely to succeed.

Given the encouraging findings outlined here there would seem to be a strong case to increase the focus on alcohol consumption as part of routine consultations in primary health care settings and at hospitals. There are, of course, associated costs of staff time and resources in carrying out these screenings, but the results, which indicate that, in this case, a brief intervention of information-giving and general advice seems to be as effective as more in-depth interventions of counselling, are encouraging. These findings clearly can not be generalised to that portion of the population who already have clearly identified alcohol-related health and other problems which will require a much more specialised intervention.

Such specialist interventions include psychotherapy, chemical treatments, aversion therapies, and the use of support groups such as Alcoholics Anonymous. Comparison of outcomes from these various interventions is extremely problematic, in particular in measuring 'success', relapse rates and so forth. It is beyond the scope of this chapter to consider such treatments.

Different programmes may have either abstinence or controlled drinking as their aim. Abstinence means what it says; controlled drinking is much more difficult to define. Comparisons of the outcome of interventions with these different goals suggest that certain problem drinkers may be able to continue as controlled drinkers. Those most likely to succeed as controlled drinkers are relatively young, socially stable, have had only a brief history of alcohol-related problems and have not suffered major withdrawal symptoms (Sarafino, 1994).

A group who have been recently targeted for alcohol reduction interventions is college students. In the United States, between 70 per cent and 96 per cent of students drink alcohol and it is estimated that as many as 25 per cent of them could be heavy drinkers. Strikingly, young college women are drinking almost as heavily as men. The provision of information to this group has been effective as an intervention and more concerted strategies are now being tried to reduce consumption. A programme developed by Marlatt and his colleagues has included information provision, the acquisition of skills to moderate drinking, the use of drinking limits, relaxation training, nutritional information, aerobics, assertiveness training, and almost anything else you might think of. Since the consumption of alcohol in this group of people is highly affected by peer influence and social situations, much of the interventions have considered ways in which these aspects can be more readily modified. Students are encouraged to follow a 'lifestyle rebalancing' (Marlatt and George, 1988) where the student begins to think of him or herself as health oriented.

SMOKING TOBACCO

Britain still has the highest mortality rates in the world for all the major smoking-related diseases: lung cancer, ischaemic heart disease and chronic obstructive airways disease. These diseases are also characterised by irreversible damage and short life expectancy following diagnosis. Smoking accounts for over one-third of all deaths in middle age and 11 per cent of all deaths in the UK (Heath Education Authority, 1991).

In a recent survey of tobacco smoking, Jarvis (1994) comments that smoking tobacco is unusual among drug dependencies for a number of reasons, including that its prevalence and trends have been well charted over a number of decades and across a number of different countries in the developed world. Furthermore, he shows that there is a range of reliable quantitative indicators of smoke intake, such as for example salivary cotinine, which indicate that smokers' self-reports of intake and use are accurate and reliable. We can therefore accurately chart changes in the profile of tobacco smoking. During the late 1940s and 1950s almost 80 per cent of men in Britain were tobacco smokers and there was no obvious social class difference. By 1990, however, 31 per cent of men and 29 per cent of women smoked cigarettes (Smyth and Browne 1992). There has also been a marked change in socio-economic gradient associated with smoking. Sixteen per cent of professional men and women were smokers in 1990, but 48 per cent of unskilled men and 36 per cent of women in manual occupations. Age, before retirement age, is no predictor of smoking status for men, but it is for women, where higher rates of smoking are associated with younger age. Jarvis also argues that smoking is linked directly with poverty, independently of its link with social class. Finally, smoking is strongly correlated with alcohol consumption.

Learning to smoke

Beginning to smoke, or 'recruitment', has obviously and unsurprisingly received the greatest amount of attention from researchers. Many of us know from bitter personal experience or from the testimony of others that, once established, the smoking habit is remarkably difficult to end. It is most appropriate, therefore, that preventive work should be targeted at young people before they embark on a smoking career.

The onset of smoking typically occurs in the early teenage years in Britain. Goddard (1992) describes a study of secondary school children who were interviewed three times in 1986, 1987 and 1988 when they were between the ages of 12 and 15. The aim of the study was to see which factors were most closely associated with children starting to smoke. At the age of 11 in Britain only 1 per cent of children describe themselves as 'regular smokers'; by the age of 15 this percentage has increased to more than 20 per cent. This study therefore tried to track children through this 'risk period'. Goddard describes the risk factors or pre-existing characteristics that were best predictors of who began to smoke, and these were:

- being a girl
- having brothers or sisters who smoke
- having parents who smoke
- living with a lone parent
- having relatively less negative views about smoking
- not intending to stay on in full time education after the age of sixteen
- thinking that they might be a smoker in the future.

(Goddard, 1992: 17)

All these factors are independently associated with starting to smoke. Goddard also suggests that smoking is not a well thought out behaviour and is highly opportunistic in nature. She suggests that early smoking education needs to take account of different levels of smoking experimentation and address the gender difference. It is not at all clear what is the basis for this gender difference; many studies now show that it exists, however. Goddard suggests that girls, although showing the same degree of experimentation as boys of this age, were more likely to become smokers as a result of the experimentation, were more likely to describe themselves as dependent at lower levels of consumption and had lower self esteem, and saw themselves as less socially skilled than boys. Which, if any, of these factors are contributors to the gender imbalance is difficult to estimate. Goddard concludes by arguing also that a pricing policy might be the most effective way of reducing opportunistic consumption in early teenage years; and the banning of the sale of cigarettes in ones or tens could also have the same effect.

Townsend (1993) contends that a pricing policy in combination with other measures could cut cigarette consumption by half. She suggests that this could achieve a smoking rate of only one person in five by the year 2000. This is obviously a highly controversial approach. Raising cigarette prices would directly affect those on low income, perhaps pushing them even further into the poverty trap. Townsend counters this argument by reminding us that an unskilled manual worker is five times more likely to die from lung cancer than a professional man. It is an interesting debate but one that should remind us that interventions tailored only at the level of the individual may sometimes not be the most effective way of achieving health changes.

Very few studies have addressed smoking in countries beyond the first world. Tobacco companies are targeting sales directly at countries such as those of Southern Africa, and as yet there are very few health messages getting through. There is the additional complication that some countries, such as Zimbabwe, have tobacco has a major cash crop, earning valuable foreign currency. Health education messages in this context are likely to be doubly unpopular and difficult to deliver.

Why smoke?

So while we know a good deal about *who* starts to smoke, we still know remarkable little about *why* smokers start to smoke. Although there now must be few people in the western world who do not know about the dangers of smoking, there may still be aspects of how this knowledge is applied to oneself personally that are of interest. It is entirely possible to know that something is a risk (a volcanic eruption, for example) and yet not feel oneself personally at risk (they don't happen here). Chapman *et al.* (1993) examined differences between smokers and ex-smokers in terms of their cognitive dissonance reducing beliefs, otherwise known as self-exempting beliefs. Respondents to a postal questionnaire in Australia were asked to indicate whether they agreed that smokers were more likely to be at risk of six diseases. The diseases were heart disease, poor circulation, bronchitis, lung cancer, stroke and rheumatoid arthritis. All but the last are known to be smoking related; the last was included to test response bias. Forty-two per cent of ex-smokers but only 28 per cent of smokers agreed with the risks of smoking and these diseases. No difference was found between smokers and ex-smokers in their perceived risks of rheumatoid arthritis, hence no response bias was apparent. A series of self-exempting beliefs statements were also used. Examples would be: 'I think you have to smoke a lot more than I do/did to put yourself at risk', and 'Most lung cancer is caused by air pollution, petrol fumes, etc.' Once again smokers differed significantly from ex-smokers in their endorsement of such self-exempting beliefs. We see here a clear example of how information or knowledge does not exist in a vacuum, but is mediated through personal beliefs systems that may well undermine the basic health-related message.

As with alcohol, there is a role for the general practitioner in helping current smokers to quit. Richmond and Anderson (1994) estimate from a number of studies that very brief advice from a GP can achieve a smoking abstinence rate of between 5 and 10 per cent. This is obviously very small, but given the equally small investment of practitioner's time involved, it may well be an extremely cost-effective way of helping some people stop. Sanders *et al.* (1993) carried out an intervention study at general practice surgeries in Oxfordshire. More than 4,000 smokers were randomly allocated to an intervention or a control group. The intervention group were invited to see a practice nurse for a health check that included advice on quitting smoking. Only 26 per cent of those invited attended for the check; of these, 66 per cent were women. Following the intervention, there was a one month and one year follow-up. At one month, 11 per cent reported that they had stopped smoking; and at one year 13 per cent reported having stopped smoking. Clearly this study can be considered only from the point of view of those people who were sufficiently health conscious to attend for a check up. The fact that two-thirds of them were women is also important, since there is no indication in the study of how this compares with the original sample invited to attend. Nevertheless, there is some room for encouragement that a brief health check might be useful in helping some people stop smoking. What was particularly interesting about the study was that it was possible to predict during the initial health check who would be successful in quitting smoking. Nurses' ratings of smokers' motivations to stop were a good predictor of both initial and sustained cessation. As the authors say: 'The important practical question is how nurses use this information – should they target support at the motivated or spend more time encouraging less motivated smokers?' (Sanders *et al.*, 1993: 1704). We still do not really know what to do for the best to aid the cessation of smoking.

A striking fact is that around 80 per cent of those who do stop smoking do so without any artificial aid or intervention from another person. Most ex-smokers are likely to cite will-power as the main ingredient to achieve smoking cessation. They also report having tried and failed to quit once or twice, or sometimes more, before their successful attempt. I am not sure whether this is heartening news or not for smokers.

Aids such as nicotine patches and chewing gum are now becoming widely available. There is some evidence of short-term addiction but overall they seem to be a useful adjunct to the inner strength required. A meta-analysis of controlled studies considered the effectiveness of nicotine gum. (Lam *et al.*, 1987) When used in smokers' clinics, the use of nicotine gum improved cessation from 13 per cent (placebo) to 23 per cent (nicotine). Their analysis of trials comparing brief advice plus nicotine gum with advice and no gum concluded that the gum enhanced cessation rates from around 5 per cent to 9 per cent. Nicotine patches are a more recent tool; Foulds (1993) summarised a number of studies and concluded that patches can roughly double the success rate in general practice settings. Once again, though, we are looking at changes from 5 per cent to around 9 per cent – a great improvement, but with still a great distance to go. Nicotine replacement therapy, either by patches or gum, is a useful adjunct to brief interventions but much more is needed (including the elusive will-power variable) to account for substantial changes in smoking patterns in the UK.

An expert report on Women, Smoking and Low Income (Graham, 1993) begins by exploring a paradox – that the poorest members of the community, those whose health is adversely affected by social and economic disadvantage and who therefore have the most to gain from not smoking, compound their risk by making unhealthy choices about the way they live. Smoking amongst women is related to their ethnic status (white women are more likely to smoke than Asian or Afro-Caribbean women); to their socio-economic status; to their employment status (where those who are unemployed are more likely to be smokers than those in employment) and to their marital status (those who are widowed, divorced or separated are more likely to be smokers than those with a male partner). The common factor that links these facts is that of low income. Why, then, are precious resources spent on cigarettes? Cigarettes are regarded by the women as necessities, as 'something for myself' in a life where most money has to be expended on others, most usually children. The report quotes a mother who says: 'It's the only thing I do for myself' Another says: 'It's my one luxury'. Cigarettes also provide a means of coping with life and its hassles: 'smoking stops me getting so irritable'. Under these circumstances, giving up smoking can seem an impossible task, and once again we can see how priorities other than a long and healthy life have come into play.

EXERCISE

We are constantly urged these days to engage in exercise, which is seen by health psychologists and others as having major benefits to health. There is increasing evidence that level of physical exercise is associated with the incidence of coronary heart disease; however, only aerobic exercise, that is exercise of high intensity and relatively long duration, is regarded as beneficial in reducing heart attacks and improving cardiovascular functioning. Exercise is also seen as having the effect of reducing poor habits such as drinking and smoking. Taylor (1995) reviews evidence that suggests that by the age of 80, the increase in life expectancy due to exercise is almost two years; she also reminds us that an 80 year old would have spent virtually two years of that life in exercise.

The Theory of Reasoned Action and the Theory of Planned Behaviour have been applied to exercise behaviours in a number of studies. Blue (1995) reviews twenty-three studies mainly considering young to middle-aged people. She suggests that the findings show that the theories could be useful in identifying psychosocial determinants of exercise behaviour; changing beliefs about how exercise can influence the intention to exercise. Once again, however, there is rarely a measure of exercise behaviour itself, and there is rarely a follow-up over a period longer than a few weeks.

There is some evidence that exercise is associated with good mental health as well as physical health. Biddle and Murtrie (1991) review the evidence from a number of large-scale surveys and cite Stephens' (1988) conclusions:

> The inescapable conclusion . . . is that the level of physical activity is positively associated with good mental health.

Mental health is considered, in this context, to be general feelings of well-being with infrequent episodes of depression or anxiety. Depression is reported to be significantly improved by regular exercise. There appear to be gender differences here with more women reporting relieved feelings of depression. The counterpart is that exercisers report increased irritability, guilt and tension when missing their usual level of exercise. In a comparison of marathon runners, joggers and non-exercisers, Wilson *et al.* (1980) found that the two exercising groups reported lower scores on depression, anger and confusion scales; and that marathon runners had more positive mood profiles than joggers, which is depressing for the non-exercisers. Most of these studies tend to be correlational and the association of positive mood and physical exercise is exactly that – an association rather than a causal agent. Attempts to show the causative link have been problematic. Biddle and Murtrie review studies where regular exercisers are deprived of exercise and compared with regular exercisers who continue in their normal schedules. The deprived group show reductions in positive mood. However, the reviewers comment on the difficulty in getting exercisers to give up their routines and the risk of selection bias in recruiting subjects into the two groups.

The effects of physical exercise as a buffer against stress have been extensively studied. Crews and Lander (1987) carried out a meta-analysis on thirty-four studies and concluded that subjects who were aerobically fit had a reduced response to psychosocial stressors and had a somewhat faster return to normal after a stress-inducing experience. Such evidence has encouraged many health professionals, including GPs, to 'prescribe' exercise to those who complain of depression and anxiety.

The benefits of exercise have been studied in an interesting project by Patterson et al. (1988). They unobtrusively observed families during a day out at a zoo. Half the families had participated in a twelve-month intervention programme to modify diet and increase exercise levels, while the other half had not. During the day, the target group walked further, ate less and more healthily than the control families, which suggests that the modification had generalised into everyday living. This is one of the few studies in which attempts have been made to move beyond both self-report of behavioural change and obviously 'monitored' exercise tests.

Given these health benefits, why is it that the usual place for the exercise bike to be found is in the loft and that leotards and exercise videos gather dust in a cupboard? Adherence to exercise programmes is notoriously difficult to achieve: 'the best predictor of regular exercise is regular exercise' (Taylor, 1995). The first three to six months are apparently critical to the process of becoming a regular exerciser; if the habit can be established for at least six months, then it is very likely to continue. One of the main reasons given for failing to exercise is lack of time. Dishman highlights the necessity of exercise being readily accessible and convenient (Dishman, 1991). Age is also important, with a definite fall-off in the amount of exercise undertaken as middle age approaches. Women in particular report fear of injury as a major deterrent at this time of life. A study in 1992 by Sallis et al. examined triggers to beginning exercise. They found that self-efficacy was a strong predictor of uptake of exercise for both men and women. Men, though, were also affected strongly by environmental stimuli such as availability of exercise equipment and facilities; women on the other hand were influenced by social variables such as support from others. This is a clear example of how strategies to encourage exercise need to be targeted carefully and modified accordingly.

CONCLUSIONS

This has been a long chapter, yet there are other major areas of interest that have not been covered in it, most notably the effects on health of diet, of weight reduction, and of illegal substance use. These are three examples of topics that have clear preventive themes. However, what should be clear from this chapter is that individual decisions about aspects of our lives can directly influence our health status. Also, that to some extent, the power to improve our health lies in our own hands. Later chapters, however, will consider health in wider settings, where decisions affecting our health are often not within our immediate control.

Chapter 5

Sexual health

INTRODUCTION

It would be impossible to encompass the range of work that has been carried out in the past ten years as part of the general strategy to prevent the spread of HIV/AIDS. No single chapter, let alone a sub-section of one, could review this work in full; hundreds of articles have been published in psychological journals each year since the pandemic became apparent. I shall to try sketch very briefly the development of preventive work in this area and then see how far we can go in assessing it.

There are really two stories about the way in which our awareness of the threat of AIDS grew. The first story is now well documented via Randy Shilts' book *And the Band Played On* and by the film from that book; there have also been a number of plays, for example *The Normal Heart* (Kramer, 1993). These show the way in which early cases of HIV/AIDS went unrecognised and how slowly the severity of the problem began to be acknowledged. They depict the prejudice that resulted from the early definition and awareness of it as a 'Gay Plague' that mainly, if not exclusively in those days, affected gay men. The mobilisation of gay men and other groups to form a coalition to gain public and official acknowledgement of the threat is well documented and the furore over who was the 'discoverer' of the AIDS virus.

The second story was taking place in Africa. Africa has both been blamed as the source of AIDS and ignored by the rest of the world in terms of its concern about AIDS; we consider this aspect further in Chapter 8. Approximately two-thirds of those with HIV are in the African sub-continent. The first (controversial) cases identified were in Kinshasa, Zaire, in the 1950s. It probably began to be widespread during the 1970s, but was identified only in 1983. The vast majority of people with HIV/AIDS in sub-Saharan Africa have acquired it via heterosexual intercourse; the ratio of men to women is approximately equal. The age of onset of AIDS in sub-Saharan Africa is typically in their early twenties for women and in their late twenties, early thirties for men.

What both these stories share is a recognition that we need to understand far more than we do about sex: how it is negotiated, perceived and experienced by women and men. There is still very little knowledge that is reliable since the subject matter is regarded as unfortunate and certainly unappealing to the electorate. There is also an acknowledgement that condoms would be effective barriers to the transmission of HIV/AIDS, as they would to the transmission of other sexual diseases. Survey after survey shows that people are well aware of the protection offered by a condom. Why then, are they used so infrequently?

I will try to offer some background to the general area of sexual health which will help us to understand what might be done to help prevent sexual ill health. First, though, we need to consider why so little is known about this major feature of human behaviour.

The opinion that there is something not very 'nice' about researching and discussing sex pervades much work in this area. We do not, in most cases, attribute the characteristics of a person's research interest to themselves – choosing to study slugs does not make you one – but choosing to study sex carries with it all sorts of connotation and expectations. One's interest may be described as 'voyeuristic' or 'prurient'. One's friends invite one to consider researching in 'nicer' areas and one does not discuss findings too loudly at parties.

STUDYING SEXUAL BEHAVIOUR

Early studies

Until the publication of Kinsey's surveys in 1948 and 1953 there was little systematic evidence concerning aspects of sexuality. These early reports have been heavily criticised, quite rightly, for inadequate sampling and problems with the interview techniques. Nevertheless, they provided the bench mark for much more recent research and, until recently, were the only large-scale sources of information on many aspects of sexuality such as homosexuality. Pioneering work on sex and sexuality was also undertaken in the mid to late 1950s by William Masters and Virginia Johnson. They set up a laboratory to undertake a scientific investigation of human sexual responses. Their early work was concerned with physiological responses of humans to sexual stimulation, and the work was published in 1966 as *Human Sexual Response*. Possibly because the work was potentially so controversial, Masters and Johnson focused on physiological and biological aspects of the sexual response, whilst downplaying, if not totally ignoring, the social and cultural aspects. Nevertheless, their laboratory-based research facilitated the development of scientific discussion about sex.

Ford and Beach published a book in 1952 – *Patterns of Sexual Behaviour* – that considered the sexual behaviour of humans and 'lower animals'. It gathered evidence from 190 different societies to show both the similarities of sexual behaviour and the variations between groups. The authors were acutely aware of the climate in which they were writing. They concluded: 'It is most regrettable that an area of inquiry having such fundamental importance in both its practical and its theoretical aspects should have been so inadequately studied and so incompletely understood' (Ford and Beach, 1952: 287).

Recent studies

It would be encouraging to be able to write that our study of sexual health and sexual behaviour in recent years has not suffered from the problems outlined briefly above. The emergence of HIV/AIDS provided, if it were needed, an obvious justification for the further study of sex and sexual behaviour, since the degree of ignorance of such matters was apparent in the scientific community as much as in the general population. Thus, in the United Kingdom, concerns about sexual health provided the impetus in 1987 for the commissioning of the British National Survey of Sexual Attitudes and Lifestyles (Wellings *et al.*, 1994), originally supported by the Health Education Authority (HEA) and the Economic and Social Research Council (ESRC). This quasi-governmental support was withdrawn from the project, however, following concerns expressed by Mrs Thatcher and others as to the propriety of spending public money in this way. Fortunately, an independent charity, The Wellcome Trust, stepped in to fund it and thus allowed the project to proceed. This is a clear illustration that, as late as September 1989, sex was still felt to be a subject that was 'too hot to handle'.

There are then large areas of behaviour concerning sex that remain largely uninvestigated. This lack of research was based on three assumptions: that to ask such questions may not be 'nice', that people may refuse to discuss sex with researchers, and that if they did reply, what they said could not be relied upon to be the truth.

The National Survey of Sexual Attitudes and Lifestyles was the first study in Britain that systematically attempted to break down these taboos and provide reliable and valid evidence about sexual behaviour. It aimed specifically to assist health care professionals working in many areas of sexual health care; but it also had other objectives such as stimulating 'further social inquiry in this field, addressing questions raised by previous research and posing fresh ones by generating new hypotheses' (Wellings *et al.*, 1994: 14).

Because of the methodological challenges associated with work in this area, careful decisions had to be taken about methods of data collection and modes of inquiry. It was decided to place a lower age limit of 16 on the sample. This decision is represented as being taken to ensure 'that a sizeable proportion of young adults would already be sexually experienced' whilst protecting 'sexually inexperienced respondents from being asked questions that are not relevant to them'. I suspect that these statements also mask the extreme difficulty in undertaking research on sexual matters with young adolescents. There is still an ideologically-based approach that considers that to discuss sexual matters with 'inexperienced' youngsters may somehow or other push them into becoming sexually active. I can find no evidence whatsoever to support this assumption; what it means in practice is that if you want to do research on sex you need to tread with extreme caution around the early age issue or you may run the risk of being unable to do any research at all.

The upper age limit set by the survey is also interesting. The upper age limit was set at 59 years. The justification for this decision is two-fold – first that it was suspected that older people would find the questions overly intrusive and would be less willing to respond; second that people over this age were not significantly at risk from HIV/AIDS and other STDs ('many of the topics . . . are known not to affect older people greatly'). In the context in which this survey was undertaken, both decisions are probably appropriate. It is sad though that we still know so little about young and old people and their sexual behaviour.

Face-to-face interviews were carried out on a random sample by 488 trained interviewers. In all, 18,876 interviews were completed on a sample that was broadly representative of the British population. As such, it represents an enormous achievement in helping us to understand sexual behaviours. A number of themes were covered by the survey and there is space here to cover only a few which can serve to indicate the range of preventions possible and necessary to secure sexual health.

Age and contraception at first intercourse

The National Survey reports extensively on the age of first intercourse from among their respondents. They comment on the ease with which such an event is recalled, implying that it had, and continues to have, significance for an individual. Fewer than 1 per cent of the sample claimed to be unable to recall it (Wellings *et al.*, 1994: 35). The data show a steady decline in the age at first intercourse; among women aged 55–59 at the time of interview the median age at first intercourse was 21 years, while for those between 16 and 24 at time of interview, 17 was the median age. The same trend is found for men, with men between the ages of 55 and 59 reporting 20 as their median age, while those between 16 and 24 reporting 17. There are educational differences apparent here: compared with those with graduate education, non-graduate men are three times more likely to have had sex before their sixteenth birthday, and non-graduate women are twice as likely. 'Only one in four male graduates had experienced sexual intercourse before the age of 18 compared with more than half of non-graduates' (Wellings *et al.*, 1994: 53).

The use of contraception at first intercourse has also improved over the decades. Failure to use contraception at first intercourse was reported by fewer than a quarter of the women and a third of the men aged 16–24. But the likelihood of using contraception is also related to age. If intercourse takes place below the age of 16 then nearly half of women and more than half of young men report no contraception. Over 16 and these proportions change to 32 per cent and 36 per cent respectively. Reasons for this failure to contracept on the part of those under 16 are likely to be complex – they may find greater difficulty in getting contraceptive supplies, or their sexual activity may be less planned; whatever the reasons, it is clear that this age group is particularly vulnerable to unwanted pregnancy. Condoms are the most frequently used method of contraception at first intercourse, with 47 per cent of men and 50 per cent of women using them; this compares with under one-third of respondents in other age groups reporting condom use. This would argue for the 'unavailability' hypothesis since condoms are the contraceptive method most readily available outside medical settings; it would also support the 'unplanned' hypothesis since they would also be the only contraceptive method available outside 'office hours'. Condoms are also now, though, clearly associated with safer sex, i.e. protection from STDs as well as safety from unwanted pregnancy. Alcohol is strongly related to lack of contraceptive use (Wight, 1993), with evidence again for the 'unplanned' hypothesis.

Patterns of sexual partners

There is great variation between the number of sexual partners that different people have at different times of their lives, and how many partners they have. While many people report relatively few partners; some report considerably more (Johnson *et al.*, 1989, 1992). Patterns of partner change are of great significance in understanding the transmission of STDs, including HIV. Holmes and Arral (1991) showed that the risk of acquiring an STD increases with the number of sexual partners with whom an individual has unprotected sex, and that the spread of STDs is strongly influenced by the extent to which the small group of multiple-partnered people mix with those having fewer partners. Johnson and Wadsworth (1994) examine the National Survey data from this point of view. They report an extremely skewed distribution, with 65 per cent of men and 77 per cent of women reporting no or one sexual partner over the last five years. At the other end of the scale, 1 per cent of men reported more than 22 partners and 1 per cent of women more than 8 partners during the same period. Maximum numbers of reported lifetime partners exceeded 4,500 for men and 1,000 for women. Johnson and Wadsworth comment that there is a marked preference to report in multiples of ten when respondents are reporting multiple partners; this suggests that there is a large error associated with these very higher figures (imagine being number 876 for example!). There is also marked variability in the number of partners across the age group, with those in the 16–24 bracket reporting the greatest number of sexual partners – 21 per cent of women and 20 per cent of men in this age group reporting more than ten partners in the last five years. This bears a clear relationship with the highest incidence of reported STD's which occurs in those aged 20–24 (PHLS, 1992). There is also the consistent phenomenon that men report higher numbers of partners than women. Other surveys, such as Johnson *et al.*, 1990 and Wadsworth *et al.* 1993 have found this. A survey by Knox *et al.* (1993) reports an average of 6.20 partners for men and 3.90 partners for women over a lifetime, but 'a lifetime' beginning in the 1960s is obviously different from one beginning in the 1930s.

There are few, if any, equivalent surveys in Africa. It is asserted that it is extremely difficult to ask personal questions about sex, which is traditionally a taboo subject in many African societies. This should not deter social scientists from attempting such studies. Many of us who have worked in such areas of research have learned that it is not so much *what* is being asked about but *how* it is asked and *who* is asking, that makes a study successful (or not). We will not be able to make progress in prevention and intervention without the basic knowledge that surveys such as those described above are now providing. A survey of current knowledge by Standing and Kisseka (1989) reviewed what work there was and reported almost no systematic research on sexual behaviour in

Africa. They point to the considerable variation across the continent in patterns of sexual behaviour, attitudes and beliefs. Marriage practices continue to undergo major changes, and data on adolescent sexuality suggests high rates of sexual activity amongst young people beginning at a very early age (as young as 9 or 10 years old). In this context, work on HIV/AIDS needs to be culturally and ethnically specific.

Commercial sex

The extent to which men pay for sexual encounters with women remains poorly understood. As Johnson and Wadsworth point out 'the role of prostitute–client contacts in the spread of STD's has through the centuries been a repeated subject for social and moral debate, but seldom the subject for scientific study before the advent of AIDS' (Johnson and Wadsworth, 1994: 119).

Commercial sex workers in Africa have been fairly widely studied (Wilson *et al.*, 1991a, 1991b; Ngugi, 1988) although there are major problems in identifying individual women as 'prostitutes'. A few women may use commercial sex as their sole income, but many others may supplement a meagre income from elsewhere with occasional commercial sex; still others may be wholly dependent on one or more men for support but not identify themselves in any general way as prostitutes. 'Girlfriends' in urban Africa are an integral part of the social scene, at all levels of society. They operate against a background of migrant labour. Men go to urban areas for work and are separated from their families left in the rural areas for months at a time; under such circumstances, urban girlfriends may have similar relationships to those that many women have with their husbands. David Wilson has been working with single women in many areas of Zimbabwe and Zambia encouraging the use of condoms. His methods involve peer education that is designed to provide education and support at grass roots level for women to continue to protect themselves against STDs and HIV/AIDS. There are a number of such projects. The success of them is difficult to evaluate directly; however, Wilson and others report that there are reductions in rates of STDs following such interventions and that these reductions are maintained over a period of time, sometimes for as much as three years. The major characteristic of research such as this is that it is not a short sharp shock of an intervention where 'experts' zoom in, intervene, and zoom out again. By working via peer education there is a greater chance that long-term change in risky patterns of sexual behaviour may be achieved. In this context it is worth considering Wilson's commentary on the project: 'Our experience is that prostitutes are among the most responsible people where sexuality is concerned anywhere in society, immeasurably more so than men' (Wilson *et al.*, 1991b).

Johnson and Wadsworth (1994) in the UK survey asked a single question concerning the payment of money by men for sex with women. Clearly this is a very restrictive account of commercial sex, but may be informative in so far as it goes. In their answers, 6.8 per cent of men reported ever paying for sex, and 1.8 per cent had done so in the past five years. Age and marital status were important in predicting likelihood of ever having paid for sex in this group. Older men who were widowed, separated or divorced were significantly more likely than married men (but not cohabitees) to report having had sex with prostitutes. A history including a homosexual partner at any time was also associated with raised odds of commercial sex with a woman. Others have also reported that women in the commercial sex industry may encounter a relatively high number of bisexual men (Bell and Weinberg, 1978). Travel away from home is also likely to be important as a predictor, as it is in migrant worker groups in Africa.

Knox *et al.* (1993) suggest that in a town such as Birmingham, with a population of 1.1 million persons, there will be approximately 1,000 prostitutes at any one time. They estimate that street prostitutes may have an average of 22 clients per week. In their survey of 2,530 people, 6.4 per cent reported having had sex with a prostitute during their lifetime; this is a remarkably similar figure to that reported above. They found that reported use of prostitutes was age related, with an especially high level amongst men aged 45 years or more. They suggest that this is an important effect, and that younger men are using prostitutes less.

Sexual health education interventions

Health education has targeted interventions in sexual health towards young people who are identified as being particularly 'at risk'. There are several studies that point to very low levels of knowledge and understanding, particularly about STDs (Abraham *et al.*, 1991; Mellanby *et al.*, 1992). Oakley *et al.* (1995) report the outcome of a systematic review of sexual health education intervention studies. Using stringent criteria for evaluation they identified only twelve 'sound' studies that had been carried out, of which only three were judged by them to be effective. The results of these studies suggest that in order to be effective, interventions need to be based on what young people say they want in sexual health information and resources; they should focus on changing behaviour rather than simply on knowledge or attitudes, and that an adequate follow-up period is essential in order to consider short-term and long-term effectiveness. Oakley *et al.* lay out clearly the 'ground rules' for good evaluations of interventions that should be followed in the future.

CONTRACEPTION

There have now been numerous studies on the avoidance of pregnancy. Much of the research has been carried out on a small unrepresentative group – unmarried females, often college attenders or attenders at family planning clinics. A survey of the literature by Sheeran *et al.* (1991) identifies them also as being white, never married, middle class and between the ages of 13 and 25. Males have hardly been studied at all, and there is little recognition in the literature that birth control may be a joint decision.

Several studies have highlighted the important gaps in young people's knowledge about contraception. A study in 1983 found that 52 per cent of the men they interviewed and 37 per cent of the women could not identify the time in the menstrual cycle when pregnancy risk was greatest. Knowledge is not the only barrier to effective contraception. Attitudes towards sexual activity remain negative. Lowe and Radius (1987) found that 17 per cent believed that females who carried condoms with them would be deemed to be promiscuous.

Condom use

Weller (1993) carried out a review of studies to determine the effectiveness of condoms in reducing HIV transmission. He reviewed a number of studies of which some had sample sizes too small to detect an effect. His conclusions from studies from which he could combine the data led him to conclude that condoms had an effect on HIV transmission of around 69 per cent. This is encouraging, if not unexpected, news; why then are condoms used so irregularly?

Thomson and Holland (1995) carried out a qualitative investigation of 150 young women between the ages of 16 and 21 in Manchester and London. They were interested in identifying their sexual knowledge, practices and the meaning of these. Young women understand 'safer sex' to be, almost to the exclusion of anything else, the regular use of condoms, and 77 per cent in Thomson and Holland's survey responded 'yes' to the question 'would you be willing to ask a partner to use a condom in the future?'. Yet only 23 per cent of the same sample had ever used a condom. Clearly the matter is complex and Thomson and Holland identify three sets of constraints that operate to make condom use problematic. These are: 'the existing contraceptive culture, the symbolic meaning attached to condoms and their own lack of power, autonomy and control within sexual situations' (Thomson and Holland, 1994: 19).

The first set of constraints concern the current contraceptive culture in which oral contraceptives are the most common form used by young women. In this survey the pill was used by 24 per cent of the young women. It is seen to be reliable and 'hidden' from the actual sexual encounter. The widespread availability and use of the pill has also shifted the balance of responsibility for contraception to the woman. 'Spontaneity' is considered an important feature of sexual interactions, and the pill accommodates to this model well. Thomson and Holland argue powerfully that spontaneity is oppositional to condom use:

> The image of sex as spontaneous relates strongly both to romantic images of sex as being 'swept off one's feet', as it does to a lack of confidence about and knowledge of their bodies. The 'rational' safer sex messages ('you know the risks, the choice is yours') can be seen as antithetical to an ideology of femininity which constructs sex as relinquishing control in the face of love.
>
> (Thomson and Holland, 1995: 21)

The symbolic meaning of condoms

Condoms carry a variety of symbolic meanings. They are particularly associated with 'casual sex', with 'one night stands' and with first sexual encounters. All of these meanings mitigate their regular use in longer-standing relationships. Thomson and Holland outline the, by now, well-charted contraceptive route from early condom use to 'progression' to the pill as the relationship becomes established. This is compounded by the need to define a relationship as 'steady' or 'serious' to oneself and others as a more culturally approved form of sexual behaviour than casual sex. Going on the pill fits well with this definition; condoms do not. Some recent campaigns have attempted to socialise the condom by catchy slogans like 'tell him if it's not on, it's not on'. But this raises the issues of power and control in sexual relationships, which we will consider next.

Power autonomy and control in sexual situations

Pressure within sexual encounters was found to be present in 26 per cent of this sample. Many of the young women's objections to using condoms centred around fears of their partner's disapproval. 'For a young woman to insist on the use of a condom for her own safety requires resisting the constraints and opposing the construction of sexual intercourse as a man's natural pleasure and a woman's natural duty' (Thomson and Holland, 1995: 24).

I have quoted extensively from this qualitative study to illustrate the complexities involved in the 'decision' to use a condom. Many studies (I could list more than seventy) have investigated combinations of variables as predictors of condom use; many models have been adapted to account for variation in condom use. This work has its place; however, the level of predictive validity of many studies is extremely low. An example would be the work of Moore et al. (1993); here we see an attempt to predict the use of condoms during a sexual encounter. Questionnaires were distributed to a group of adolescents inquiring about their attitudes towards condoms and their intentions to use them at their next sexual encounter. Respondents were then asked to return a questionnaire after their next encounter that indicated whether or not they had in fact used a condom. Very little was found strongly to predict condom use, although many variables proved significant in statistical analyses. The availability of a condom at the time of sexual intercourse was the single most important variable. This is hardly surprising, but does emphasise that psychological dimensions of individual's decisions such as 'intentions' need to be supported by basic aspects such as having condoms readily available to young people when and where they may be initiating sexual encounters. Mahoney et al. (1995) tested the ability of the Health Belief Model and self-efficacy to predict condom use by college students. The Health Belief Model was inadequate in explaining multiple patterns of condom use. Only one factor, assertiveness, which they consider to be part of the self-efficacy construct, was effective in distinguishing sporadic users from non-users and consistent users of condoms. Once again, the social context of the sexual encounter proved to be an important predicting variable, the sporadic condom users had more sexual partners and were drunk more often when engaging in sexual intercourse.

Finally, it is worth considering the context in which many young people can acquire contraceptive supplies and advice. A recent study carried out in the West Midlands interviewed providers of contraceptive care to young people. Interviews were conducted with general practitioners, school nurses, community medical officers and practice nurses, all of whom came into regular contact with young people, mainly young women, seeking contraceptive care. Many of the interviewees spontaneously expressed concern about the age at which first intercourse was taking place and about the nature of teenage sexuality. They voiced expectations that early sexual activity would come to be source of regret as the young people 'matured', and expressed strongly held beliefs that young people could not handle the emotional aspects of sexual relationships. One medical officer asserted that young people 'had lost their values. . . . There's no shame in it any more. There's no prizing your virginity'. Such attitudes are probably not unusual, and probably also reflect society's views on early sexual activity. However, in the context of a service that is specifically aimed at providing contraceptive advice to young people, such attitudes and beliefs are likely to transmit a negative and judgemental approach by staff to teenage sexual needs (Pitts *et al.*, 1995).

PREGNANCY

One of the latest 'moral panics' concerns teenage pregnancies and abortions. *The Health of the Nation* (DoH, 1992a) includes a target for reducing pregnancies in young women under the age of 16 from a rate of 9.5 per 1,000 to 4.8 per 1,000 by the year 2000. This is perhaps a surprising target since less than 1 per cent of all pregnancies are to girls under the age of 16 (Peckham, 1993). Pregnancy during teenage years is described as a 'problem' by both researchers and public health educators. Sharpe (1987) offers a more useful way of considering the issues by pointing out that teenage mothers have lives that are 'quite different to those of other girls of the same age without children'. The incidence of teenage pregnancy is unevenly spread over different groups of teenagers with those of lower socio-economic class and those who are black being most likely to be 'at risk'. This is especially true in the United States, but similar findings are reported also for the UK (Moore and Rosenthal, 1993).

There are two accounts that are usually offered to account for why teenagers become pregnant. The first account suggests that they perceive some material gain from the pregnancy, usually housing or financial benefit. Whilst this account is increasingly driving policy decisions about welfare provision in the United States there is little evidence for it. Phoenix (1991) considers several British studies and finds no evidence for this as a motivating factor; and Moore and Rosenthal also find no evidence in studies in Australia and the United States. The second account suggests 'incompetence' as the primary reason for adolescent pregnancy and this finds support in research such as that reported by Phoenix that 82 per cent of adolescent girls had not 'planned' to get pregnant. A large number of studies suggest that the notion of adolescent 'invulnerability' has a part to play in the explanation of teenage conceptions. A sizeable proportion of teenagers do not regard themselves as likely to conceive, even though they are having sexual intercourse.

Peckham (1993) reviews the wide range of studies that have examined preventive approaches to teenage pregnancy. She categorises the preventive approaches into three groups: those that impart knowledge or influence attitudes, those that provide access to contraception and those that enhance life options. Taking the first category first, there have been numerous studies in the United States and Sweden that suggest that sex education may influence contraceptive use. Sweden has one of the lowest teenage pregnancy rates in the word and 5–15 year olds have a better sexual education than their counterparts in Britain or the United States. Peckham suggests that such studies 'suggest that more openness about sexual issues can result in lower conception rates' (Peckham, 1993: 129).

The reasons why some teenagers are better prepared than others for sexual encounters is multifactorial. Evidence suggests that higher academic expectations, greater ego strength and self-esteem all predict decreased likelihood of teenage pregnancy. The role for preventive programmes is relatively under-developed in this area. What is most apparent is the lack of research or interventions targeted at young boys. It is as if girls become pregnant without the aid of boys at all. This severely limits what we can understand about the personal and social situation in which intercourse between teenagers is occurring.

SEXUALLY TRANSMITTED DISEASES

Remarkably little work has been done on the psychological aspects of STDs if the mountain of information about HIV/AIDS is put to one side. Often surveys of knowledge, attitudes and behaviour do not distinguish between different STDs and ask general questions that are applicable to some, but not necessarily all, STDs. The situation has improved recently with the growing awareness of the risks, especially to young people, from untreated STDs. In the United States around two-thirds of STDs occur in people under the age of 25. The most recent surveys of HIV/AIDS confirm that knowledge about the virus is high; very little is yet known about young people's knowledge of other STDs.

Certain population groups are particularly at risk from STDs, such as the Aboriginal communities in Australia. Surveys have shown that both gonorrhoea and syphilis are endemic in many of these communities. Bowden (1995), in a review of Aboriginal communities in the Northern Territory, reported gonorrhoea as 'so common in young, sexually active people that it has almost become normal to suffer an episode'. He estimates that rates of untreated STDs amongst Aborigines are twenty-five times higher than the Australian national average and the health consequences of such rates are alarming – problems of pelvic inflammatory disease, infertility, ectopic pregnancy, foetal death and premature labour are all common consequences of STDs. Health promotion programmes that do more than simply impart knowledge of risks are essential. Bowden points to the epidemiological synergy of STDs and HIV as an indicator that future HIV/AIDS is likely also to be located in these communities.

These findings have their parallels in work in sub-Saharan Africa where the presence of an existing STD can increase the risk of transmission of HIV. A recent study by Moses *et al.* (1994b) in Kenya reported that the prevalence of STD's in the antenatal population was in excess of 20 per cent. The length of time that individuals are infected before they seek treatment is an important determinant of transmission. If sexual activity continues after an individual has been infected, then the opportunity to transmit the disease is great. There is a complication in that many STDs are asymptomatic, especially in women. Thus, two issues are important: general education, which might encourage some form of routine screening for STDs, and information about the dangers of delay in treatment seeking after symptoms appear.

The most common presenting symptom reported in Moses *et al.*'s study was vaginal discharge for women and urethral discharge for men. The significance of such discharges therefore needs to be addressed in any educational campaign. Moses reports that 12 per cent of men in his sample and 38 per cent of women had continued to have sexual intercourse after such symptoms had begun to be apparent. This difference between men and women is likely to be a reflection of who initiates the sexual encounter and who can decide or refuse to continue with the sexual encounter. The power to initiate sexual intercourse rests largely with men: they can decide not to continue to have sex after they have noticed the symptoms; women cannot. This account is supported by Moses' finding that married women were more likely than unmarried women to continue to have sex whilst symptomatic. Most of the married women thought they had acquired the STD from their husbands.

These findings have parallels with a recent study carried out in Zimbabwe (Pitts *et al.*, 1995). We studied women attending a general health clinic in the capital, Harare. We were particularly interested in talking with women who had been infected with STDs more than once. Our findings from these women were that 97 per cent thought they had acquired the STD from their husbands. The same percentage of the men interviewed reported they had acquired the STD from a girlfriend or casual or commercial sexual partner. Women also reported being unable to discuss their infection with anyone else; the stigma of infection was too great for them. Men were able to discuss their infections with other men and received some support from them.

Recently we have studied undergraduates in the UK to examine their knowledge and beliefs about STDs. Most undergraduates are surprisingly ignorant of basic information about all STDs with the exception of HIV/AIDS where their knowledge base is extensive. It is of concern that most do not draw parallels between HIV and other STDs. Predictors of relatively good knowledge of STDs were various and unrelated either to gender or sexual experience.

A study by Ogden and Harden (1995) examined the beliefs and attitudes of teenage school pupils surrounding condoms and their use. What is of interest for us here is that whilst 67 per cent of the 12 and 13 year olds identified the function of a condom to prevent pregnancy, and 49 per cent to prevent the transmission of HIV, only 33 per cent identified a function to prevent the transmission of STDs.

CONCLUSIONS

The area of sexual health is one that is now the subject of a great deal of research. Social scientists are able to ask questions of the general population, and sometimes of young people, which will enable them to design prevention programmes to protect against pregnancy, HIV and other STDs. But all is not now unproblematic. There are still areas that are extremely difficult to study, most especially young people. Schools and health authorities are reluctant to support or even to allow such research and are fearful of the unfortunate media attention that has concentrated on sex education classes, which have been perceived as going beyond what is acceptable.

Tamsin Wilson summarises the problem:

> Combine the stultifying British 'reserve' about sex and sexuality with the political ascendancy of a New Right determined to halt the steady liberalisation of social attitudes . . . and you have a social climate tailor-made to ease the passage of a sexually transmitted virus.
>
> (*The Higher*, 23/6/95)

Chapter 6

Psychoneuroimmunology

There has long been the idea that there are interrelations between the mind and the body, and that one can affect the other. The idea is embodied in recent research that attempts to relate the three domains of psychology, neuro-endocrinology (encompassing both the brain and the central nervous system) and immunology (which considers the body's defences against bacteria and viruses). Psychoneuroimmunology (PNI) is the inelegant term that describes this work. PNI is beginning to allow us to view the relationship between mind and body in a new and complex way. This chapter will outline some of the great volume of recent research that has sprung out of this approach. First, though, we need to consider the nature of the immune system, and hormonal responses to stress.

THE IMMUNE SYSTEM

The human immune system is the body's means of defence against 'invaders' such as viruses. It is fundamentally a system of defence against foreign material; its function hangs on an ability to distinguish *self* from *non-self*. It is not located in any particular part of the body but is distributed throughout to involve almost all the organs. It is fortunate that the immune system is not located in any single part because micro-organisms can attack the body throughout any part of it; the response to infection therefore has to be flexible and mobile. The lymphatic organs are primarily involved in the immune system; these include bone marrow, lymph vessels, the thymus gland and the spleen. There are two kinds of immune response – a non-specific and a specific response. The non-specific response involves phagocytes – these will consume and hence destroy almost anything. For many infections the production of antibodies is the key to the body's defences. Specific immune responses are involved in producing antibodies to fight specific invaders; antibodies slow down an invader to allow the phagocytes to destroy them, and they act as a memory to identify the invader if it has been encountered previously. Cell-mediated immunity involves T-lymphocytes (T cells), which are the infection-fighting white blood cells. Their activity level is taken as a key indicator of how effectively the immune system is functioning. There are three main types of T-lymphocytes: helper cells, suppresser cells and natural killer cells (NK cells); there are also memory T cells, which retain a memory of an invader.

It has long been known that the immune system can go wrong and can even turn against the body's own tissues. It can begin to make antibodies to its own tissues; this is referred to as auto-immunity. Some diseases are thought to have an auto immune basis, for example rheumatoid arthritis. More recently, it has been thought that the immune system plays an important part in the control of cancer; as recently as 1982, however, a major textbook of clinical immunology made no mention of the effect of psychological stress on the immune system (Baker, 1987)

ADER'S CONDITIONING STUDIES

In the 1970s Robert Ader was carrying out conditioning experiments with rats. He was feeding rats both an unpleasant-tasting drug and saccharin within a very short time of each other. The conditioning study was to show that the rats associated the saccharin with the drug and subsequently learned to avoid the saccharin. Unfortunately for the rats, during the period in which they learned to avoid the saccharin they began to die, and the more saccharin they drank, the quicker they died. Now saccharin is not a poison, so what was going on? Ader himself says: 'I'm a psychologist, not an immunologist – I didn't know there were no connections between the brain and the immune system'. He therefore fell free to postulate connections between the mind and the immune system. The drug that had been associated with the saccharin was a suppressor of the immune system; Ader reasoned that the rats had learned a conditioned response to the saccharin that also lowered the immune system. Ader and Cohen have since shown that conditioning can work on a wide range of immune system responses such as B cells (cells that produce antibodies), T cells, NK cells and macrophage cells (Ader and Cohen, 1985; Ader et al., 1991). Gorczynski and colleagues have shown that rats can also be conditioned to enhance their immune responses (Gorczynski et al., 1982). These animal studies have pointed the way to understanding the development and course of a number of different diseases. Perhaps, the reasoning goes, some psychological disturbance has caused the immune system to turn on itself and hence, perhaps, some psychological occurrences have triggered an auto-immune disease such as rheumatoid arthritis. It is a small step from this to consider that perhaps it is also possible to prevent or to slow down the development of such a disease, again by influencing psychological state rather than by directly intervening in the body. There has been a lot of postulation in this discussion; links and causes are still only tenuously suggested. Overall, the evidence from animal studies suggests that there is a link between stress and suppressed immunity. In particular, it would seem that the state of helplessness is immunosuppressive.

PSYCHOLOGICAL FACTORS INFLUENCING THE IMMUNE SYSTEM

What becomes of the broken hearted?

In 1884 an article in the *British Medical Journal* suggested that at funerals: 'the depression of spirits under which the chief mourners labour at these melancholy occasions peculiarly predisposes them to some of the worst effects of chill' (quoted in Baker, 1987). The first convincing demonstration of this link between bereavement and a depressed immune system was a study by Bartrop *et al.* (1977). They compared the spouses of patients who were fatally ill or who had just died from illness with matched controls. The experimental group of bereaved spouses showed a significant impairment of their immune response to the introduction of a substance that stimulated immune reactions. This finding seems to explain the well-known fact of increased bereavement in spouses within six months of their loss (Parkes, 1986). Schleifer *et al.* (1983), in a prospective study, showed that bereavement produced significantly lower levels of immune response when compared with pre-bereavement scores.

Stroebe (1994) points out that in an age of postmodernism 'it is no longer fashionable to die of a broken heart'. She examines the evidence to account for why bereaved people are more likely to die than the non-bereaved. She suggests that two factors underlie this phenomenon: the first factor relates to the direct effects of grief – the broken heart hypothesis. These effects are linked with increased depression, loss of attachment and less romantic constructs such as guilt and dependency. The second factor she associates more clearly with the stresses of a bereavement. She considers both the physiological underpinning of the stressful event and the change in role and function that usually follow a bereavement. She suggests that these factors must interact to explain the pattern of results she describes, and concludes: 'When extreme grief coincides with severe life stresses during bereavement, the risk to life is likely to be greatest of all.'

Studies such as these have often used life event scales to assess the degree of stress experienced by an individual in the months prior to the onset of an illness. Measuring life events such as these presents considerable problems. Early attempts, such as the Holmes and Rahe Life Events Scale, have been the subject of much criticism. Often the scales were drawn up by the researchers themselves and it is not at all certain that the events chosen were appropriate for the sampled populations. They typically ignored non-events (not being promoted at work is surely traumatic), and some of the events were confounded with their consequences (divorce and depression, for example). Another major source of criticism was that the scales were unidimensional – they considered the *quantity* of life events in a given period, not the *quality*. However, the major difficulty with the studies was that they were frequently retrospective in design. Researchers would probe people about their life events record after they had become ill. This raises problems of recall accuracy, and the possibility that people are motivated to find causes or explanations for their current state of health. Even the more recent prospective studies face a similar problem, since they often involve the same process of trawling a past period, typically six months, prior to a follow-up.

Most studies now would attempt a prospective design to begin to overcome some of these difficulties. Studies by Kiecolt-Glaser *et al.* (1984) related immune activity to feelings of loneliness and social isolation. Medical students had lowered NK cell activity during an examination period compared with a month before the examinations. Those medical students also reporting loneliness had even lower NK cell activity. Similar relationships were also found for psychiatric patients.

A recent study by Glaser *et al.* (1993) focused on the Epstein Barr Virus (EBV) which has been shown to be critically controlled by immune competence. Kiecolt-Glaser *et al.* studied EBV positive medical students one month before, and during, a stressful set of examinations. They measured the students' specific immune response to EBV, via blood samples. They found lowered response during the examination period, indicating a drop in immune system functioning associated with the stress of the examinations. Interestingly, they divided their students into two groups according to how active they were in seeking social support during this period of stress. Social support might be sought for a number of reasons: for example, some might seek the company of others for emotional reasons – for emotional support, understanding, sympathy or simply just to give vent to feelings – whilst others could have more instrumental reasons for seeking support – to gain advice or information about the examinations, for example. Both these kinds of social support were measured via COPE (Carver *et al.*, 1989). COPE is a multi-dimensional coping inventory that measures both situational coping and dispositional coping via thirteen sub-scales. These two kinds of social support seeking identified in Kiecolt-Glaser's study were found to be highly correlated (0.74) and so a single measure of social support was used. Subjects who scored above the median on COPE were found to have higher levels of antibodies to EBV, which is interpreted as more loss of control over the virus. Greater social support seeking was also associated with higher stress reports and greater loneliness. Thus the role of social support, and certainly the role of social support seeking, remains problematic.

Kiecolt-Glaser *et al.* also examined the quality of a relationship and how that would affect the smooth functioning of the immune system. They studied the quality of relationship in married couples and couples whose marriages had broken down. For both sexes better marital quality was associated with less depression and with a better immune response (Kiecolt-Glaser *et al.*, 1987; Kiecolt-Glaser and Glaser, 1988).

CANCER, STRESS AND IMMUNITY

The first scientist to suspect that the immune system is involved in the control of cancer was William Cooley working in the United States in the early part of this century. But for fifty years the hypothesis that the growth and spread of cancer was influenced by the immune system fell from fashion. Then in the 1970s a substance was discovered in the blood; one of its functions seemed to be the destruction of tumours. This was known as the Tumour Necrosis Factor (TNF). It damages the blood vessels that feed a tumour, starving the tumour of oxygen and causing it to die. In addition, it stimulates T cells that cooperate to destroy the tumour. Increasingly, there is support for the hypothesis that psychological events can influence the immune system, which in turn will influence the likelihood of cancerous growth.

Some of the most striking evidence has come from Steven Greer and his colleagues. Greer *et al.* (1979) provide evidence from a study of women with breast cancer. They followed a group of 69 women with breast cancer at five and ten year markers to try to distinguish survivors from non-survivors in terms of their measured adjustment to breast cancer three months after they had received their diagnosis. They found that short survivors were most often hopeless and helpless and that some were stoic in their adjustment. In contrast, long survivors showed 'a fighting spirit'; using a coping strategy of 'denial' also correlated well with long survival. The study claimed that, particularly at ten years after diagnosis, outcome was independent of any biological factor that might have affected it. DiClemente and Temoshok (1985) offered some support for this finding. Looking at patients with malignant melanoma they found women who had stoic acceptance and men who displayed strong hopelessness/helplessness had an increased risk of disease progression. There have, however, been critics of the work who have pointed out that crucial information about the degree of cancer spread was not taken into account. Furthermore, Cassileth, in a similar study, but not a replication study, failed to find these differences (Cassileth *et al.*, 1985). From the point of view of preventive health, it is important to establish whether different psychological attributes exist prior to a cancer diagnosis that might account for the onset of the disease. Such research is extremely difficult to carry out. Greer and Morris (1975) report a study that compared 160 women admitted to hospital for breast tumour biopsy. Interviews and testing were carried out one day before the operation. A comparison of data from those women who were found by operation to have breast cancer and those who were not showed personality differences associated with the degree to which emotion was released. In particular, failure to release anger was found significantly more frequently among women with cancer than controls. Similar results were reported by Geyer (1993), who studied 33 women with cancer, 59 with benign tumours and 20 with gall stones. Using a life events scale, Geyer reports more severe life events for those women with cancer. Most particularly, he identifies events associated with loss as being more likely to be reported by women suffering from breast cancer than women in the other two groups. In the 'malignant' group the severest events were four times more likely than in the controls. Cooper *et al.* (1986) carried out a large-scale prospective study on 2,163 patients attending breast screening clinics. They report that women subsequently diagnosed as having cancer had suffered significantly more loss or illness-related events than controls. There are, though, other studies, including those of Greer *et al.*, which have failed to find any relationship between loss events and the development of cancer.

Herbert and Cohen (1993b) carried out a meta-analysis of the literature linking stress with depression. They considered up to thirty-five studies that offered suggested links between mood state and immune state. Clinical depression was reliably associated with large alterations in cellular immunity. Such immune alterations were more pronounced in hospitalised and in older patients. Their summary of the findings suggests that there is a greater reduction of NK cells following 'objective' stressful events. They also claim that longer-term, naturally occurring stressors such as bereavement have a greater effect on the immune system than short-term acute stressors.

McGee *et al.* (1994) carried out a meta-analysis on seven longitudinal prospective studies of depression at time 1 and cancer mortality and morbidity at time 2. These wide-scale and long-term epidemiological studies are helpful in assessing cancer risk. The first study is known as the Johns Hopkins Precursors Study (JHPS); this is an investigation of around 1,300 medical students, the large majority of whom were male. They were initially assessed at time 1 between 1948 and 1964; by 1979, fifty-five of them had developed cancer and they were compared with matched controls. Twenty-two per cent of those now suffering cancer had reported depressive feelings at time 1 compared with 7 per cent of the controls. A similar study of men working in Chicago, known as the Western Electric Health Survey (WEHS), followed men for twenty years and reported 9.5 per cent of the depressed group had died of cancer compared with 5.3 per cent of the non-depressed group.

A third study is the controversial Cvrenka study. This is a cohort of 1,353 men and women from what was then known as Yugoslavia, mostly aged over 50 years at time of first interview. Ten years after the initial study 204 were identified as having cancer and their early levels of depression were significantly linked with late cancer risk. This study, however, has been heavily criticised on methodological grounds outlined by McGee *et al.* (1994).

The McGee meta-analysis combined studies excluding the Cvrenka study and found some evidence 'on the borderline of statistical significance' that an early history of depression or depressive symptoms predates later onset of cancer. However, only three of the studies entered into the meta-analysis comprised women and men, and other characteristics of the samples were very different from each other. Furthermore, evidence from epidemiological studies tells us something about the different rates of cancer, but very little about the individuals who are at greater or less risk.

In this area, the jury is certainly still out. The evidence remains confused and such studies and their implications in themselves generate great emotion. It is clearly crucial to know whether existing personality traits might affect disease onset or progressions, whether life events have any predictive validity in the development of cancer, and whether different response and coping styles might influence disease progression. It seems that the evidence favours an interpretation that does link these attributes to cancer, but caution is important at what is still an early stage in the debate.

HIV AS THE TEST CASE

Human immunodeficiency virus (HIV) is clearly a problem that can shed light on this relationship between immune system deficiencies and the mind. Attempts to determine whether certain psychological states, life events or personality traits are associated with disease progression have produced very mixed results. Certain studies, most notably those of Coates (1989), Kessler et al. (1991) and Perry et al. (1992) have found no relationship between stressful life events and symptom onset in HIV infection, between stress reduction and immune function in gay men with HIV, and between psychosocial variables and lymphocytes. Nevertheless, there is also a body of evidence that does claim such relationships exist. The work of Antoni et al. (1991) and Margaret Kemeny and her associates (Kemeny, 1991; Kemeny et al., 1994) offers some support that active coping style and depression are linked to HIV progression. Her most recent work suggests that a pattern of responses to AIDS, which she labels 'realistic acceptance', is strongly related to decreased survival time. Men with low realistic acceptance scores survived on average nine months longer than men with high realistic acceptance scores. This construct bears marked similarities to the 'stoic acceptance' identified by Steven Greer in his work with breast cancer patient. Kemeny postulates that 'realistic acceptance' may determine survival time by immunological mediation. It is crucial to this argument, however, that other mediating factors, such as engagement in 'risky' behaviours such as high alcohol or drug consumption, or lack of engagement in health protective behaviours, are not also linked with realistic acceptance. This is a debate that raises emotions very quickly on both sides. The stakes are high – quite literally, people's lives depend on the outcomes of research such as this. What is encouraging is that these difficult and methodologically challenging studies are being carried out.

PERSONALITY FACTORS AND STRESS

The relationship between stress, a lowering of the immune system and illness is a complex one. One of the important variables to consider from the point of view of preventive health is the role of personality differences in the process. An example of the kind of factor thought to be important in determining this relationship is that of hardiness. This was first studied by Kobasa and also by Maddi (with Kobasa). In her original study (1979) Kobasa studied middle-aged American business men for a period of three years. They all completed the Holmes and Rahe Life Events Schedule initially to determine their degree of life stress prior to the study. Kobasa identified and monitored two groups that had experienced equivalent high degrees of stress, but one group tended to develop illness and the other didn't. The difference between the two groups was a personality characteristic she defined as 'hardiness'. Hardiness involves three components: commitment, control and challenge. People showing high commitment tend to have a large degree of involvement with life; they throw themselves into whatever they are doing; people high in control tend to believe they can influence events and feel they have control of much of their life; people regard events as providing opportunities for challenge rather than threats. 'Hardiness', the combination of these three rather disparate factors, distinguished between sick executives and healthy ones. There has been some support for the role of this personality characteristic in preventing illness (Ganellen and Blaney, 1984; Kobasa et al., 1985). However, there are some significant problems with both the construct and its application. The correlation between the three defining characteristics is, at best, weak; and one or two may be present without the third. The early research was severely limited in its generalisability – the reactions of middle-aged American executives to what are self-defined stressful events may be very different from other groups of differing age, gender, ethnic group and social and economic status. For example, executives may genuinely have more opportunities to respond to events by seeking to control and challenge them. Funk and Houston (1987) found significant correlations between hardiness scores and general maladjustment.

Alfred and Smith (1989) found a clear relationship between neuroticism and lack of hardiness, and also suggest that the degree of maladjustment is what is predictive of illness, rather than a particular personality style of coping with stress. Funk and Houston also claim that only retrospective studies support Kobasa's hypothesis and that prospective studies show no effects. The problems associated with using life events scales such as that of Holmes and Rahe have already been considered in this chapter.

Nevertheless, the idea of individual differences in reactions to stressful life events remains an interesting one. Other contenders for the role of key defining personality characteristic have been 'a sense of coherence' (developed by Antonovsky, 1987), and optimism (Scheier and Carver, 1985). This latter characteristic has been increasingly studied in relation to reactions to major illnesses such as breast cancer. Its role seems to be to act as a prompt for certain kinds of coping rather than others.

Friedman and colleagues have recently (1995) reported on an extension of one of the best-known and comprehensive studies in psychology, which was first begun in 1921. Lewis Terman recruited 1,528 'bright' Californian boys and girls and studied their intellectual and psychosocial development into adulthood. These 'Termites' have now reached old age and many of them are dead. Friedman *et al.* gathered and coded their death certificates and studied those who were still living. They achieved a sample size of rather more than 1,000. They found, as is consistent with other studies, that the women in the sample tended to live longer than the men. Friedman's main areas of interest, however, concerned childhood personality and its impact on longevity. He constructed six personality dimensions based on Terman's trait ratings of the children from parents and teachers. Friedman reports that childhood social dependability or conscientiousness predicted longevity and that this was a predictor independent of smoking, drinking or injury measures. Friedman also found that childhood optimism – as measured by cheerfulness and a sense of humour – was inversely related to longevity. The more cheerful children died earlier than their gloomier counterparts. This goes against much of the research cited earlier. However, Friedman's analysis suggests that cheerful children are more likely to drink, smoke and take risks later on. Friedman suggests that cheerfulness is a useful strategy when coping with stress such as impending surgery, but harmful if it develops more generally into carelessness. Overall the study supports the position that suggests that aspects of individual psychology are significantly related to longevity, across the life span. In particular the area that has often been referred to as 'ego strength' aspects, such as dependability, trust and lack of impassivity, are predictors of a long life. The combination of personality characteristics and social stress factors are likely to be interactive as well as independent factors.

So far we have looked at long-term effects of stress or disposition on health; there is, however, another strand of research, which considers the immediate impact that daily stresses can have on health.

REACTIONS TO ACUTE STRESS

One line of research has been to consider the role that short–term acute stressors may have in illness patterns. It has often seemed a more promising approach to consider minor upsets on a day-to-day basis and to attempt to link them to minor ailments, rather than to try to assess the long-term consequences of more chronic stress. This approach allows for a more immediate assessment of events and their significance, and a more immediate consideration of symptoms. Furthermore, the tracking of daily events and their outcomes may have greater ecological validity than experimentally induced stress. The inevitable choice from amongst the minor illnesses was the common cold. The cold may be common but it is not insignificant in its consequences and there is also little prospect of a cure. The Medical Research Council's Common Cold Research Unit was established after the Second World War specifically with the purpose of finding the causes and a vaccine for the dreaded disease; it was closed down in 1990. Mrs Thatcher was not impressed with its record of success. Some of the work at the Common Cold Research Unit identified individual differences in susceptibility to infection. Broadbent *et al.* (1984) and Totman *et al.* (1980) showed that introverts were more likely to develop colds, as were individuals who had just experienced major life events. Individuals who performed poorly at a given task are also more likely to develop colds subsequently. More recently, Cohen *et al.* (1991) provided solid evidence of the link between colds and stress. The subjects were 154 men and 266 women who were volunteers at the Common Cold Research Unit. All subjects completed a series of self-report questionnaires that measured their degree of psychological stress. They were also given three personality measures that tapped self-esteem, personal efficacy and extroversion. Subjects were then inoculated with either a cold virus or a saline placebo. Somewhat surprisingly (for us cynics) none of the subjects injected with the placebo developed colds; 38 per cent of those exposed to the virus developed colds. There were interesting differences amongst those who had received the cold virus. Highly stressed persons had higher rates of colds. In particular, those people who reported stressful life events were reliably more susceptible to colds. Scales measuring perceived stress and negative affect did not reliably predict cold susceptibility. How to measure a cold, though, can be problematic; mucus weight is one (unattractive) possibility; another is temperature. Cohen *et al.* offer data which link average daily temperature following a cold virus injection with stressful life events.

They reported no relationship between stressful life events and pre-virus exposure temperature but as can be seen from Figure 6.1 there is a reliable difference after the cold injection.

The role of personality remains ambiguous. Cohen *et al.* (1993) report no reliable associations between introversion–extroversion, or personal

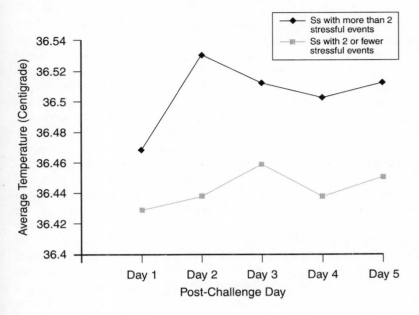

Figure 6.1 Stress and the common cold. Average post-challenge daily temperature (degree centigrade, adjusted from baseline) for infected subjects (n=325) with two or fewer stressful events and subjects with more than two stressful events

Source: Cohen *et al.*, 1993. Copyright 1993 by the American Psychological Association. Adapted with permission.

efficacy and colds. There is though a small association between decreased self-esteem and increased colds. Thus the earlier work of Totman and others seems unsupported by this study. There remain a number of problems with the interpretation of these results. *Number* of life events seems a crude measure that takes little account of the impact of any particular life events on an individual. A divorce might be responded to differently if it is messy, bloody, amicable, or long overdue. There seems room still for more 'naturalistic' studies of upper respiratory infections, which might shed light on the meaning of minor life events in the scheme of things.

There have been a few studies that have adopted similar methodologies in the search for the link between colds, immunity and stress. A recent American study (Stone *et al.*, 1987) set a methodological frame-work which was then adopted by Evans in a series of studies. The first study (Evans *et al.*, 1988) involved sixty-five undergraduates over nine weeks; thirty subjects provided complete records for the entire period. Subjects were required to provide a daily report on an Assessment of Daily Experiences Form. It had three sections, the first of which incor-porated a twelve-item mood scale. The second comprised a twenty-nine-item events schedule. These events covered the range of work- and study-related events ('under a lot of pressure from impending deadlines', for example); leisure-related events ('group or club meeting'); family- and friends-related (sickness of relative or friend) and another category; there was also the facility to write in events not covered by the twenty-nine items. Each event was also rated for its desirability and meaning-fulness. Finally, there was a symptom checklist of fourteen common symptoms and six questions concerning health for that day. Through this weighty questionnaire it was hoped to build up a very detailed picture of subjects' daily activities, their personal significance, and the subjects' daily health. The following measures were obtained for each subject on each day: a total for desirable events, a total for undesirable events, and the presence or absence of an illness episode. An illness episode was defined as two or more consecutive days with a set of symptoms consistent with an episode of infectious illness of the upper respiratory tract (a cold).

Analysis centred on the four-day period prior to the onset of an illness episode, and this event period was compared with a control period of four days that did not precede an illness episode. The control period was carefully matched for each subject in that it was calculated from the same days of the week as the precursor days to avoid confounding with weekly event frequencies; there is typically a higher frequency of desirable events at weekends, for example. Analysis of variance of frequency of desirable events found that precursor days contained significantly fewer desirable events than equivalent control days. Figure 6.2 shows the mean number of desirable events on days prior to illness episodes compared with equivalent control days.

The most pronounced dip in the data comes at Day 4, with much less difference on Days 5 and 6. This finding mirrors the study by Stone *et al.* (1987) who also reported four days prior to illness onset as the critical period for decrease in desirable events. No similar significant differences emerged for the undesirable events.

There could be an alternative account of the reasons for this dip: subjects may feel somewhat unwell just before the start of a cold and hence reduce their intake of pleasurable activities. This account does not

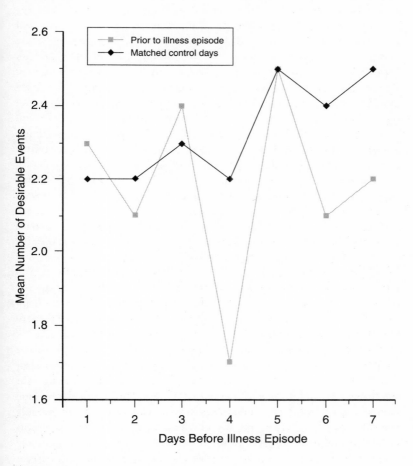

Figure 6.2 Desirable events and the onset of a common cold

Source: Evans *et al.*, 1988. With kind permission from Elsevier Science Ltd, The Boulevard, Langford Lane, Kidlington OX5 1GB

explain the particular dip four days prior to onset of cold – this interpretation would predict a gradual decline through the precursing four days, not the pattern both Stone *et al.* and Evans et al have observed. The dip four days prior to a cold may reflect a time when viral attack of the mucosal surfaces coincides with a temporarily lowered efficiency of the immune system. This is part of the growing body of evidence that links psychological, neurohormonal and immunological responding.

In a study of mood states and minor illness (Evans and Edgerton, 1992), mood and health reports from sixty-five administrative and clerical staff were obtained daily over a period of ten weeks. They completed questionnaires to assess daily mood, a checklist of sixteen common symptoms, and specific questions on seven common disorders. Factor analysis of the mood scores generated three factors, which are labelled: happiness (playful, elated, energetic and leisurely); tense depression (tensed-up, concentrating, tired, sad) and hostile depression (sad, angry, cynical and self-centred). They report that colds significantly correlate with hostile depression and that tense depression is related to head and neck ache. The explanation offered for the development of colds is that hostile depression lowers the immune system, and this is supported by the finding that subjects reported significantly more hostile experiences on day four prior to a cold.

Stone et al. (1993) in a further study attempted to replicate and extend these studies. Seventy-nine middle-aged men completed daily records for an average of eighty-three days. Twenty-three men suffered at least one illness episode. No evidence of the four day dip was found. Evans and Pitts (1994) review the studies and try to account for the discrepancies. There are clear differences between the British studies and the ones from the US. But it is not clear why all studies prior to Stone et al., 1993 were pointing in one direction and the most recent study by Stone et al. (1994b) is not. As I write, the story continues.

These studies are, by their nature, correlational and this makes clear conclusions difficult to form. Taken together with studies involving tight experimentally induced stressors randomly assigned to subjects, the final picture is much more convincing. Stone et al. (1994b) recorded desirable and undesirable daily events from subjects and collected secretory-immunoglobulin A (sIgA) antibody; sIgA is secreted at all mucosal surfaces of the body and is linked to respiratory infections, it also serves as one of the first lines of defence to incoming pathogens, and produces immune defences to the cold virus. Because it is found in mucus it can be collected from subjects by having them spit into a container and the saliva is then analysed via an assay. Stone et al. found that reporting more desirable events was related to more sIgA antibody and that reporting more undesirable events was related to lower levels of sIgA antibodies. Desirable events also had a lagged positive effect on sIgA levels; the lag was in the order of one or two days.

So we have great consistency in the argument that stressors and the immune system are linked via psychological mood. There are, though, inconsistencies in the literature. One notable one is the contrast in findings from Stone *et al.* and Evans *et al.* that *desirable* events are of greater importance in affecting antibody levels than are negative or undesirable events. This contrasts with Cohen *et al.* (1993) and with Kiecolt-Glaser's (1984) work, both of which focus on negative stressors as crucial in predicting changes in immune functioning. It may be that in our day-to-day life, which is relatively stress free, it is the lack of desirable events that assumes importance; however, this is overridden when a major life event such as a bereavement occurs. Then, it is the strength and nature of the stressor that has a profound and much longer-lasting effect on the immune system.

The areas of stress, life events and illness have been, until now, largely concerned with the diseases of the western world – coronary heart disease, cancer and others. The models that have been generated to explain the behavioural pathogens of these diseases have also focused on limited types of stressful situation. However, the acknowledgement that we can no longer, if we ever could, conceive of the mind and the body as separate and distinct from each other is a giant step forward.

Chapter 7

Accidents and injuries

Three main areas will be considered in this chapter. These are the prevention of accidents and injuries during childhood; the prevention of accidents, most especially falls, for older people; and some elements of health and safety at the workplace. These areas have been chosen to reflect the breadth of research carried out under the umbrella of accidental injury. Accidents are a major cause of death in the UK. They are the most common cause of death in people under the age of 30. Accidents accounted for 10,193 deaths in England and Wales in 1991, of which more than 7,000 were men. For men, the major causes were motor vehicle accidents (49 per cent); 25 per cent of accidents occurred in the home. For women, the proportions were different, with 49 per cent of accidents occurring at home and 31 per cent being motor vehicle accidents (DoH, 1992a: 102). Accidents at work constitute about 4 per cent of all accidental deaths. The sections of the population most vulnerable to accidents are children, old people and those with disabilities. *The Health of the Nation* has specified targets concerning accidental injuries. These are:

- To reduce the death rate for accidents among children aged under 15 by at least 33 per cent by 2005
- To reduce the death rate for accidents among young people aged 15–24 by at least 25 per cent by 2005
- To reduce the death rate for accidents among people aged 65 and over by at least 33 per cent by 2005.

(DoH, 1992a: 104)

The government views accident prevention as relying primarily on information and education rather than being the focus of legislation, and this approach has tended also to dominate research in these areas. We will now consider further the area of accidental injuries to children.

ACCIDENTS AND INJURIES TO CHILDREN

An injury can be defined as 'the outcome of a behavior-environment interaction that leads to death or damage' (Finney *et al.*, 1993). Injuries are the major cause of death for children in most of the industrialised nations. In the United States, injuries cause about half of all child and adolescent deaths, with a gradual increase from around 37 per cent in the age group between 1 and 4 years, through to around 48 per cent for 10–14 years olds and more than 55 per cent for 15–19 year olds. Wilson *et al.* (1980) suggest that for every death due to injury there are approximately fifty hospitalisations, and extrapolates from this to consider that one in five children in the United States annually experiences a serious health problem as a result of injury. In the United Kingdom, accidental injuries are the most common cause of death for children over 1. Two hundred and forty-six children between the ages of 1 and 4 died from accidental injuries in England and Wales in 1990. An estimated 6,500 attendances at Accident and Emergency departments annually are because of childhood accidents (Kendrick *et al.*, 1995).

The causes of death also vary across the span of childhood. Finney documents evidence from a number of US sources to show that deaths of children aged between 1 and 4 years are mainly through burns, drowning and car accidents; for children aged between 5 and 9 the fatalities are from being a pedestrian or being in a car accident. For children aged above 10, the major risk is from a car accident; this risk peaks dramatically in the age group 15–19. Wilson *et al.* (1980) point out that the major causes of hospitalisations may differ from the major causes of death. Injuries such as falls, poisonings, burns, lacerations and animal bites figure large in emergency admissions to hospitals, although they rarely result in death. The consequences of these deaths and injuries have great psychological and social impact both on the children and the rest of their families.

Injury control strategies can be divided into passive and active interventions. Active preventions require individuals to engage in actions to prevent injuries, examples might be wearing seat belts or cycle helmets. Passive intervention measures require less input from the individual. Childproof caps on medicines, airbags in cars or traffic calming measures require little intervention from an individual but can have a significant impact on injury rates. Of course this dichotomy is a false one: most interventions involve both some active and some passive aspects. Passive strategies can be extremely effective. Finney *et al.* (1993) quote examples such as legislation and regulations that have reduced deaths by poisonings from household substances, effected a reduction in burns following the introduction of flame-retardant materials for children's pyjamas, and effected reductions in drownings following the compulsory fencing of swimming pools. There are, though, risks as well as benefits associated with such measures. There has been some debate about the alleged carcinogenic properties of flame-resistant nightwear (Blum and Ames, 1977); and childproof caps often seem to be adultproof as well (Pitts and Phillips, 1991).

Active prevention requires individuals to carry out measures; frequently it requires adults to carry out such measures on behalf of children. As such, it is necessary that there is a clear understanding of what is required, when and how frequently. This requires judgements on the part of parents about their children's capabilities. Peterson (1989) suggested that parents may over-estimate their children's knowledge. Wortel *et al.* (1994) reviewed educational programmes in the Netherlands aimed at reducing preschool injuries. The majority of such injuries occur in and around the parental home. There have to date been very few epidemiological studies examining the relationship between children's safety and parents' safety behaviour. Baltimore and Meyer (1968) and Sobel (1969) found no differences in storage and availability of poisons in the homes of children who had been poisoned and those who had not. Van Rijn *et al.* (1991) carried out a case control study on burns accidents in preschool children. Only three behaviours were significant predictors: having an oven door that gets hot whilst in use, storing hot drinks in flasks, and cooking on an electric rather than a gas stove. The link between these behaviours is possibly the non-obvious nature of the burning agent – a gas flame sends visible signals of heat that can act as a warning; an electric oven does not.

Wortel *et al.* outline four forms of parental safety behaviours that might be important in injury prevention amongst preschoolers. These are: educating the child about risks; supervising the child; making the environment safe for the child and giving first aid after an accident has happened. There are a number of difficulties associated with each of these behaviours. Very young children may have difficulty in understanding and calculating risks. Laidman (1987) suggests that parents often over-estimate the child's maturity. Constant supervision is an unrealistic goal for most parents and may not be best for the child's general development. Hence, some attempt to create a 'safer' environment would seem to be the most promising strategy, plus the provision of some basic education to parents about what to do following an accident.

Wortel and Ooijendijk (1988) interviewed parents of preschool children about why they were not implementing some appropriate safety measures. They found parents either thought their children too young to be confronted with the risk situation or old enough to be able to cope with the risk situation. The parallels between these ideas about 'the right moment' for conveying such information and the difficulties that parents of older children have with judging the 'right moment' for sexual health education is interesting. Eichelberger *et al.* (1990) examined parental knowledge of risks to children up to the age of 13. They found a good understanding of the risks associated with cars, but a poor understanding of risks associated with burns; most parents believed 'most burns children receive are from fires'. Glik *et al.* (1991: 300) found that mothers of preschool children under-estimated the likelihood of burns, poisoning and head injuries, as well as under-estimating hazards such as hot water, baths and electrical sockets.

Parents need to recognise not only the magnitude of the risks to their young children, but also their own role in reducing such risks. Langley and Silva (1982) found that only 39 per cent of the parents of a child who had an accident during the preschool period changed their subsequent behaviour to reduce the risk of a further accident. Most of the parents who did not change their behaviour (63 per cent) regarded the accident as 'not preventable'. Similar results have been found by O'Connor (1982) who showed that, following a poisoning in the home, most parents did not change their methods of substance storage. Some of the explanation for this might be linked to the work of Eichelberger *et al.* (1990: 287) who found that parents hold the belief that 'caution and vigilance are effective means to protect children from injuries'. This belief down-grades the role of passive interventions which are probably more effective in the long run than the impossible goal of constant supervision. The focus of this research, however, emphasises individual differences between parents and parental behaviours rather than placing the responsibility more widely on manufacturers, designers and others to provide safer environments for all citizens, including children.

Early studies of children's injuries adopted the approach of the 'injury-prone personality', noting that some children are more likely to be injured than others. The strongest behavioural predictor of injury rate is aggression, with 'over activity' also implicated. Jaquess and Finney (1994) carried out a study of children aged between 3 and 13 who participated in a summer camp for 'economically deprived' youngsters. Injury incidences were recorded from the children's parents and one year later a follow-up inventory of injuries was carried out. Fifty children were studied, eight of whom had injuries during the week of the camp. For the two-year study period (one year before camp visit and one year after)

fourteen children received medical attention for unintentional injuries –
this extrapolates to a high rate of 140 injuries per 1,000 subject years.
Other measures were also collected from the parents. Multiple linear
regression showed that a history of medically treated injury was the
strongest predictor of subsequent injury, accounting for one-third of the
variance. Earlier studies had also shown this relationship. A relatively
small proportion of children tend to account for a large proportion of the
injuries; ten of these fifty children had received medical attention in the
year before camp and seven of these ten received medical treatment again
in the year following camp. This study failed to find aggression and
conduct disorders to be significant predictors of injury, although opposi-
tion to parents did predict subsequent injury. Interestingly, no gender
effect was found for injury risk, although earlier studies found boys more
than three times as likely to be injured than girls (Bijur *et al.*, 1988).
There are significant limitations to this study, such as the use of parental
report as the sole measure of injury, but the results are fascinating in that
they suggest that strategies for injury prevention could be targeted very
much more specifically to those families identified as 'at risk' by presentation with first injury. The ethics of such targeting are, however,
problematic and the risks associated with identifying some children or
parents as at risk are clear. The parallels between accident-prone children
and injury prone workers will be examined in the last chapter.

An attempt to prevent the first, and potentially extremely serious,
accident is illustrated by a study carried out by Cardenas and Simons-
Morton (1993) in Texas. They targeted a low socio economic group of
Hispanic mothers attending a health clinic. They developed recom-
mendations by Graitcer and Sniezek (1988) to reduce water scald injuries.
These were:

1   to increase public knowledge about the dangers of hot tap water
2   to encourage parents to measure water temperature
3   to advise parents to reduce water temperature to 120F degree by
    adjusting the thermostat.

(Graitcer and Sniezek, 1988: 38)

Mothers attending a health clinic on certain days of the week were given
an informational cartoon showing two characters discussing the harmful
consequences of hot tap water and how to adjust its temperature. They
were then administered a short questionnaire on self-efficacy, intentions,
knowledge, attitudes and social desirability. Mothers on control days
received only the questionnaire. Results in the experimental group
showed higher knowledge, attitudes, self-efficacy and intentions in the

intervention group than in the control group. Obviously there was no pretesting here to provide baseline measures, nor was there any measurement of actual behaviour. Nevertheless, this is an encouraging approach to prevention of burns since it does show that a brief intervention during a waiting time can improve knowledge of accident prevention in an area that is critical for young children.

CYCLE HELMET USE

Bicycling for both transportation and recreational purposes is a healthy alternative to most other forms of transport. Nevertheless, it can carry with it significant risks of accident and injury, most especially again amongst children and young people. A number of recent studies have investigated the prevention of serious head injury through cycling by the wearing of protective head gear. A recent American survey reported that more than 60 per cent of bicycle related deaths involve serious head injuries. Recent surveys have suggested that fewer than 5 per cent of school-aged children wear cycle helmets (Dannenberg and Vernick, 1993) A case control study reported by them found that unhelmeted riders were more than six times as likely as helmeted ones to sustain a serious head injury. Dannenberg and Vernick argue for legislation (passive intervention) to promote helmet wearing by insisting that every new bicycle must be supplied with a helmet. This measure, they suggest, would eliminate barriers to ownership of a helmet, since the separate act of purchase of the helmet alone would be dispensed with; it should also lower the cost to the consumer of the helmets because of the increased demand and it would complement effectively other interventions such as publicity and educational campaigns to increase helmet wearing. Whilst superficially such legislation does have appeal, it is not apparent that the provision of helmets by itself will increase the frequency with which they are worn. A parallel could be drawn with the situation until recently where all new cars were fitted with seat belts for all seats and yet few people actually used them on a regular basis until further legislation requiring their *use* was enacted.

A study by Dannenberg and others (1993b) surveyed the impact of a law passed in 1990 in Howard County, Maryland, requiring persons younger than 16 who were riding bicycles on country roads and paths to wear an approved safety helmet. This county was compared with an adjoining one, where publicity about proposed legislation was widespread and a third county where no special initiatives or discussions concerning helmet wearing had taken place. Self-reports of helmet use were collected and direct observations were carried out in the three counties, before and after the legislation in Howard County. The proportion of respondents who reported always or usually wearing a helmet increased in Howard County from 11.4 per cent to 37.5 per cent. Corresponding increases in the other two counties were from 8.4 per cent to 12.6 per cent in the adjoining county and from 6.7 per cent to 11.1 per cent in the unrelated county. Hence the legislation had a clear effect on helmet wearing. Observations on use of helmets in the three counties showed increases from 4 per cent to 47 per cent in the target county and a much smaller increase in the adjoining county from 8 per cent to 19 per cent. In the uninvolved county, helmet use actually decreased over the same period. Note though, that even at its most effective, the majority of school-aged children were still not wearing helmets so these increases must be viewed in that light. Other studies have also reported increases, sometimes extremely significant increases, but the majority of children still do not wear the helmets routinely.

Witte *et al.* (1993) attempted to assess the specific factors that influence individuals first to purchase and then to use consistently bicycle helmets. Using the Health Belief Model as their theoretical framework they tested the effectiveness of a number of different cues to action. In a telephone survey of parents they found that the combination of perceived susceptibility and perceived severity could be combined into a single construct of perceived threat and that this consistently predicted bicycle helmet attitudes and intentions. However, the study was essentially a self or parent report and as such offered no direct measures of following purchase and use of bicycle helmets.

Moving to adult helmet use, Dannenberg *et al.* (1993a) studied use amongst adults riding alone or with others. Helmet use amongst 2,068 adult cyclists measured in the three American counties described above varied from 49 per cent up to 74 per cent in Howard County. They also found a high concordance when cyclists were together, around 90 per cent of use or non-use was concordant between pairs. This suggests that people tend to adopt behaviours similar to those of others and that if a critical mass of cyclists could be convinced to wear helmets, many (but not all) of their companions would follow suit. Dannenberg also extends this to children where the evidence is even more compelling. Children riding with helmeted other children were twenty-two times more likely to wear a helmet than when riding alone. Peer pressure clearly is an important variable for further research.

Cameron *et al.* (1994) report on changes in helmet use following a decade of health promotion in Victoria state, Australia. A law was introduced in July 1990 to make cycle helmet wearing mandatory; this followed extensive bicycle safety education, most especially in schools. This was the first state-wide legislation in the world so its effects are extremely important in helping us to understand the value (or otherwise) of passive interventions such as legislation. There was an immediate increase in helmet wearing from 31 per cent in March 1990 to 75 per cent in March 1991. The number of cyclists killed or admitted to hospital following head injury decreased by 48 per cent in the first year post-legislation and by 70 per cent in the second year. There was some reduction in bicycle use amongst children in the first year post-legislation, but an increase in adult cyclists. Teenagers remained the most resistant group to the wearing of helmets. We do not know what else the children were doing instead of bicycle riding; but the alternative activity might also have safety implications, and certainly if children reduce the amount of exercise they take by reducing their cycling then the legis-lation has not been all to the good. Note also that the drift of the legislation has not addressed the major cause of cycle accidents, that is the volume of traffic, mainly cars and lorries, on the road. Most cycle accidents involve collision with other vehicles, and, whilst the wearing of safety helmets will reduce serious head injuries, further protection for cyclists from other vehicles – such as through the provision of cycle paths and lanes – would probably have a greater effect. A colleague of mine who is a cyclist commented 'Why not require pedestrians to wear protective clothing also, in case they encounter a vehicle?'

ACCIDENTS IN OLD AGE

The Health of the Nation (DoH, 1992a) included accident prevention with particular emphasis on accidental deaths in people aged 65 years and over. The target is to reduce such deaths by one-third by the year 2000. It also includes the aim of 'adding years to life: and adding life to years'. Reducing the fear of accidents and injuries can be liberating for older people. The scale of accidents in older people can be gauged by a study by Graham and Firth (1992) in south-east London. They examined reports from 1,300 people over the age of 65 who were asked to record any accident that had happened to them in a one-month period. This sample had between them 108 accidents; around 80 per cent of these did not entail medical care, 16 per cent resulted in a visit to the GP and 4 per cent to a hospital accident and emergency unit. Prevention of accidents therefore is still something of an unknown endeavour, since we do not yet know the cause of many of these accidents.

Drivers over the age of 70 are between three and four times more likely to be involved in car accidents than those below 70. Only the age group 17–20 of male drivers has a worse record. We should probably, therefore, require all drivers to take another driving test when they reach 70, though it is unlikely that this would be welcomed or generally accepted (Howard, 1993).

HAZARDS AT WORK

Many working people are exposed to danger through their occupation. They may come in contact with hazardous substances that are toxic or carcinogenic, or they may be exposed to danger through their work site. It is difficult to link work and ill health directly since there is often a long delay between 'exposure' to a health hazard and the development of a disease. Froines and Baker (1985), cited in Winett et al. 1989, report that the major work-related diseases in industrialised countries are: lung diseases (asbestosis, pneumoconiosis), musculoskeletal injuries (back problems), occupational cancers (bladder, liver), amputations and other injuries (fractures, eye loss), cardiovascular disease, reproductive disorders (infertility), neuro-toxic disorders, noise induced problems, dermato-logical problems and psychological disorders. Approaches to health and safety at work also use an active–passive distinction. Passive measures are those that focus on the environment of the worker; active measures focus directly on the working individual. Psychologists, via human factors research, have made some contribution to improving safety at work; but many of the hazards are difficult to eliminate from the working environment. Plumbers, carpenters and joiners may be unwittingly exposed to asbestos whilst carrying out routine repairs; people working in a dry cleaning shop or a hairdressing salon may be exposed to hazardous chemicals.

As in the cycle safety research described above, one solution offered to the risks of the workplace is to wear protective clothing. However, solutions which tend to focus on protective clothing as a means of preventing harm are unlikely to be particularly successful in such environments where the hazards are not immediately obvious, or possibly even frequently encountered. Similar issues assume even greater importance in developing countries. A large number of different minerals are known to cause pneumoconiosis and many of them are mined in such countries. Examples would be the mining and quarrying of silica, asbestos, coal and graphite. Surveys have indicated prevalence of pneumoconiosis in certain industries in India, for example, to be as high as 32 per cent of all exposed workers (Ng, 1992).

One can witness asbestos mining in Africa where not only are workers unprotected at the workplace from asbestos dust, but they and their families live in close proximity to the mine and eat and breathe asbestos dust daily. Only strong political will for change can modify such events and their consequences; protective clothing or special procedures can reduce incidence but cannot eliminate risks as great as these. Oborne (1982) adopts a learning theory approach to issues of safety. He points out that behaviour that is safe is often time-consuming and requires special procedures or equipment; such behaviour is less likely to be reinforced in contrast with unsafe behaviour which is quicker and easier to perform. Safe behaviour is reinforced only rarely by an accident occurring. A useful focus for prevention might therefore be to examine ways of making safe behaviour easier, less disruptive and having reinforcing components.

OCCUPATIONAL ACCIDENT PREVENTION

Earliest studies of industrial and occupational accidents considered the role of the worker. Statisticians demonstrated that accidents were not distributed randomly among the population and that a relatively small number of people were involved in a relatively large number of accidents. Thus was the notion of accident-proneness born. This issue will be considered more fully in the last chapter; the focus here will be on organisational and environmental factors. I will try to show that the focus for accident prevention should remain at the level of the organisation rather than that of the individual. Smith *et al.* identified the following factors to be successful in promoting safety at the workplace:

- a strong concern on the part of management for safety
- a more stable work force, low staff turnover and absenteeism
- a humanistic approach in dealing with employees.

(Smith *et al.*, 1978: 83)

This approach considers the immediate causes of accidents, such as unsafe conditions or actions, to be manifestations of errors in management concerning responsibility, accountability, initiative and so on.

Analysis of accident rates in Zimbabwe shows that forestry and mining to have the highest frequency of accidents, but that the highest number of fatalities occur in agriculture, mining and transport. The total accident frequency in Zimbabwe is relatively low, although this may be a function of inadequate statistics collection, but the frequency of fatal accidents is five times higher than the average for European countries (Laitinen and Vahapassi, 1992). Frequently, outdated machinery and inadequate guards are major causes, with poor training acting as a contributing factor. Here again, a focus on prevention to an individual worker is unlikely to be effective in accident prevention.

In the safety literature there is now a broad consensus on basic measures in accident prevention. These are outlined by Laitinen and Vahapassi (1992) as a hierarchy of actions. The most effective safety action is to eliminate the hazards: changing the base of a paint, for example, from an organic solvent basis to water soluble base. A second effective safety action is to remove the individual from exposure: to allow the operation of machinery at a distance by remote control, for example. The next is to isolate the hazard: machinery guards would be an example of this. Warning signs should appear in all areas of danger and they should be specific in their warning rather than being a general 'watch out' or 'be careful' message. Instructions and training can alert workers to danger. Finally, and regarded by Laitinen and Vahapassi as the least effective safety action to take, workers can be issued with personal protection against the hazard. Once again, it should be emphasised that the most effective actions for safety can be taken by management and unions rather than by individuals at the workplace.

WORKSITE HEALTH PROMOTION

In the early 1980s there was a burgeoning of worksite health promotion programmes that sought to improve the health of workers as individuals 'on-site'. The workplace offers a number of features that are particularly useful for health promotion programmes (Cohen, 1985). Most employees go to work regularly and hence regular participation in programmes is possible; environmental supports can be offered such as workplace bans on smoking, healthy food on offer; contact with co-workers can offer the social support and reinforcement seen to be necessary for changing health habits. Finally, the health promotion programmes offered can be convenient and relatively inexpensive, both for the individual worker and the company. The specific outcomes to be achieved by such programmes are usually reduced sick leave and health care costs, and a higher quality workforce. Evidence suggests that smokers have a 50 per cent greater risk of hospitalisation and absenteeism than non-smokers and that 'alcoholic employees are absent approximately twice as much as the average rate' (Cohen, 1985).

An early survey (Fielding, 1979) suggested six areas were worthy of effort: hypertension screening and follow-up; smoking cessation programmes; exercise programmes; diet modification; alcoholism groups and car safety

programmes. The company Johnson & Johnson sponsored a health promotion programme called LIVE FOR LIFE. The goals for the programme
were 'to provide the opportunity and encouragement for Johnson &
Johnson employees to become the healthiest in the world and to control the
corporate costs of employee ill health' (Bly *et al.*, 1986).

Components of the programme are described by Fielding (1991) as:

- a health screening including consideration of health habits
- a series of health measurements
- communications programmes, newsletters and so forth
- a 'lifestyle seminar' to introduce employees to the programme
- behaviour change oriented action programmes concerning for
  example, smoking cessation, encouraging exercise, stress
  management.

Activities occur on the worksite, but usually in the employees' own
time. Fielding reports evaluations of the LIVE FOR LIFE programme
which compare Johnson & Johnson employees with workers at control
worksites. Two years after the introduction of the programme results
showed the Johnson & Johnson employees to have significantly higher
smoking cessation rates, to have greater weight reductions and to have
initiated more regular exercise programmes. These results are impressive.
However, Winnett *et al.* (1989) express scepticism about the effective
evaluation of such programmes. It is possible to use 'hard measures' such
as absenteeism and sick leave rates to evaluate the effectiveness of these
interventions from the point of view of the company or firm. It is much
more difficult to evaluate the effectiveness of such programmes from the
point of view of the individual. Even from the point of view of the
corporation, an analysis of the cost–effectiveness of the programmes
suggests that a relatively long-term investment is required to see benefits
outweigh costs.

It has been pointed out by Allegrante and Sloan (1986), amongst
others, that to focus on the individual to the exclusion of the working
environment can place health professionals in a tenuous position between
workers and management who may define 'the problem' differently. The
dilemma of conflicting loyalties raises questions about who benefits from
such workplace programmes.

The workplace can, however, be used simply as an opportunity to
communicate with a large number of people. In less industrialised countries this is particularly appropriate. There have recently been education
programmes concerning HIV/AIDS that have targeted workers. A

survey carried out in Zimbabwe in 1990 examined company policy concerning HIV/AIDS (Jackson and Pitts, 1991). Delegates from 159 companies were questioned of which 33 per cent had already developed a policy explicitly on HIV/AIDS and 61 per cent provided AIDS education at work. The form of this education was mainly in the form of talks and pamphlets; very few were carrying out an 'active' education programme. Some companies also distributed condoms free or at low cost. The thorny issue of screening workers for HIV was also considered in this survey. Ten companies indicated that they did screen for HIV routinely at the stages of employee selection; a further twelve companies carried out routine screening of the existing workforce; in all, 22 per cent of companies acknowledged some form of screening for HIV. One-third of the company delegates refused to answer this part of the survey – a much higher refusal rate than for any other questions. The outcomes of screening for HIV were clear – HIV-positive individuals were not offered employment, and very little backup was provided for those employees who tested positive. One of the most compelling arguments against employment screening is offered by Jackson (1992): the policy would exclude from employment thousands of people who might be fit for work for many years more; their years of training and their experience would be lost immediately, in countries where there is a serious shortage of skilled labour.

STRESS MANAGEMENT

Stress at work is frequently associated with poor health. Carroll and Cross (1990) investigated stress in a university setting – not a workplace universally identified as stressful. Forty-nine per cent of respondents to their questionnaires indicated that they found their jobs often or almost always stressful. Of those who reported poor physical health, 81 per cent reported experiencing stress almost always, in contrast with those reporting good physical health of whom only 28 per cent reported their jobs as regularly stressful. Nursing has been intensively studied as a profession where stress levels are acknowledged to be high. Gray-Toft and Anderson (1991) identified seven major sources of stress within nursing: dealing with death and dying, conflict with doctors and with other nurses, workload, uncertainty over treatment, lack of support, and inadequate preparation.

Research on the effects of work stress on health have often utilised Karasek's model of job strain (Karasek 1979). This model suggests that those jobs that involve a combination of high demands – such as time pressures – with low controls – such as little power to make decisions – are likely to encourage the development of physical and mental health problems. Job strain has been shown to predict levels of risk of coronary heart disease in male blue collar workers in Germany (Siegrist *et al.*, 1990, 1992) There are, though, some studies that throw doubt on this association, such as Reed *et al.*, 1989. A recent review (Adler and Matthews, 1994) points out that the majority of studies of occupational job strain have been carried out on European male workers and there may be difficulties in generalising to other cultures and groups: women, for example!

Stress is one of the most popular targets for health promotion in the workplace. Price (1986) has categorised stress management programmes as:

- aimed at the individual to reduce stressors – time management, stress inoculation and so forth
- aimed at reducing the stress response – exercise, meditation, relaxation
- aimed at increasing one's abilities to cope – task redesign
- aimed at addressing role demands – social support, goal-setting.

There are others that address the wider issues such as overload, increasing breaks from work and providing better working conditions, but most workplace stress management is directed at helping the individual to cope with the existing stressors, rather than focusing on reducing them. The 'problem' needs to be recognised and redefined as interactive; an understanding is required of both stressors and responses to stress, and this demands an understanding of a person's life situation and as well as the work situation.

A stress management training programme was developed by North Derbyshire Health Authority to assist its employees in the management of a demanding work environment. The aim was to impart a range of skills and techniques that would help prevent the development of stress-related problems in the work force. The training package comprised:

- general information about stress
- relaxation methods
- discussions on handling relationships
- the role of thinking in the experience of stress
- time management
- understanding and handling emotions.

Leakey *et al.* (1994) report the results of this programme. There were clear effects on employees' psychological well being, but not on their job satisfaction nor on their general life satisfaction. There is no report of long-term follow-up of this programme beyond three months and so its effectiveness remains unproven.

Cooper and Williams (1994) offer a checklist of organisational health. They claim that these are the characteristics of 'healthy workplaces':

- Health and Safety regulations are fully observed
- The working environment is as pleasant as possible
- Health screening programmes are available
- Healthy eating and exercise are encouraged
- Employees can discuss problems in confidence
- Communication systems are effective
- Morale is high
- There is mutual respect between management and workers
- The organisation is flexible
- Employees look forward to coming to work.

(Cooper and Williams, 1994: 246)

Cooper and Williams are not 'cockeyed optimists'; they recognise that 'organisations rarely act for altruistic reasons'. They argue that there is a relationship between a healthy workforce and success; at the moment this seems to be a claim rather than a proven fact. Let us hope, for the sake of the workforce, that the good of the employee and the success of the company can go hand in hand.

Chapter 8

Blaming the victim?

This final chapter will put the issue of preventive health into a broader context of medical care; the role of government and other policy-makers will be considered. This should serve to contextualise health psychology. Health is, inevitably, a political, social and cultural matter and the role of individual responsibility needs to be examined in these frameworks.

Blaming the victim can broadly be defined as 'justifying inequality by finding defects in the victims of inequality' (Ryan, 1976: 1). As an approach, this perspective has a long history within psychological literature and it is increasingly playing a part in current debates about health. Ryan's seminal book begins with a description of a humorous routine that depicted an American senator conducting an investigation into the origins of the US involvement in the Second World War. The sketch culminates with the senator exclaiming loudly: 'But what was Pearl Harbour *doing* in the Pacific Ocean?' (ibid.).

An equivalent sketch now might include Virginia Bottomley, Edwina Currie or some other government minister urging businessmen to take their spouses with them on overseas trips to prevent the spread of AIDS; exhorting old people to wear woolly hats to prevent hypothermia and demanding that all of us who do not live south of the Watford Gap change our eating habits. On learning that the infant mortality rate in Glasgow is several times higher than in Surrey a minister might be heard to mutter 'But what was she *doing* giving birth in Glasgow?'

A SUITABLE CASE FOR PREJUDICE?

The allocation of blame is nowhere so apparent as in a consideration of problems in Africa. There is a widespread idea that Africa somehow brings its problems on itself; that Africans cannot manage the supposedly thriving economies they inherited from colonialists. The facts are, of course, very different, but it is often convenient to consider the African continent as the cradle of all misery. The early coverage of the development of HIV/AIDS was characterised by the rush to identify the 'causes' as located in marginal groups in the West and as emanating from poverty and ignorance in Africa.

The earliest 'documented' case of AIDS is reported to be a 25-year-old former naval seaman from Manchester who died in 1959. The researchers who published data on this in the *Lancet* in 1990 concluded that the patient, who had an 'unexplained immunodeficiency and overwhelming pneumocystis and cytomeglavirus co-infection of the lung had HIV infection' (Corbitt *et al.* 1990). What did the daily newspapers make of this report? They focused on one aspect of the case history: that the man had been a seaman; and this provided the trigger for assumption and speculation:

- 'He had probably visited the tropics. But no one knows whether he had been to Africa.' (*Independent on Sunday*, 8/7/1990)
- 'There has been a suggestion that he had been to Africa, but Dr. Corbitt has since learned this might be incorrect.' (*Guardian*, 7/7/1990)
- 'Little is known about the seaman, but . . . he might have travelled to Africa.' (*The Times*, 6/7/1990)
- 'He is believed to have contracted the disease in Zaire.' (*Daily Telegraph*, 6/7/1990)
- 'He is thought to have visited Africa where AIDS almost certainly originated.' (*Daily Mail*, 7/7/1990)

A radio interview with the consultant was trailed with the message that this case confirmed theories about the origin of AIDS in Africa, although the consultant rapidly denied this during the interview itself.

The point is that not much is known about this young man; he could have visited Africa, Asia, America or indeed anywhere else in the world. The presence of HIV in his tissues probably confirms that he died with AIDS, but nothing else. Even that fact is now the subject of much dispute (*British Medical Journal*, News, 15/4/1995). His case, though, offered convenient support for theories about the origins of AIDS and its impact has been to confirm existing preconceptions about the origins and consequences of this disease. There is well-documented prejudice and discrimination against Africans who are travelling or working in Europe. Several countries now require HIV testing for African students before granting them entry or permission to study. Cyprus operates an interesting policy: 'African students and foreign cabaret artistes are tested for HIV' (Panos, 1990). Ironically, the USA, despite having the highest number of cases of AIDS, introduced compulsory screening of immigrants.

THE JUST WORLD HYPOTHESIS

Furnham outlines the basis of the beliefs about human nature that are sometimes described as the 'just world hypothesis':

> People who believe the world is a place where people get what they deserve (and deserve what they get) frequently blame victims for this misfortune by 'discovering' facts that caused the person to bring misfortune upon themselves. It is clearly a self-protective belief system which stresses the lawful rather than random relatedness among actions.
>
> (Furnham, 1988: 119)

He shows how this might be applied to health and medical conditions. Gruman and Sloan (1983) showed that ill people are viewed more negatively than well people and a later study by them compared reactions to vignettes, one of which concerned someone suffering from cancer and the other someone suffering from a heart attack. The heart attack victim was perceived less positively than the cancer victim (Sloan and Gruman, 1983). Furnham elaborates this finding to suggest that victims of less preventable and less well-understood diseases receive less derogation than victims of preventable ones. Others have looked at reactions to vignettes concerning people with HIV/AIDS and again have shown that the notions of 'innocent victims' and 'thoroughly guilty' victims underpin judgements being made.

The allocation of blame for a disease such as AIDS is a widespread phenomenon. Mann, the previous head of the WHO Global Programme on AIDS, has termed this a third level of pandemic. We all blame 'others': 'Britain has blamed African students, the USA has blamed Haitians, Africa has blamed Europeans, Japan has blamed foreigners, the French right has blamed Arab immigrants' (Panos, 1988). Randy Shilts portrayed movingly in his book *And the Band Played On* (1987) the prejudice that dominated the early years of encountering and dealing with the AIDS virus in the United States. The discourse around HIV/AIDS has always included the notion of the 'innocent victim' and, unspoken but implicit, the 'thoroughly deserving victim'. Freddie Mercury, from the pop group Queen, fits the second scenario neatly. The obituaries for Mercury dwelt extensively on his wayward lifestyle as a moral lesson to us all. The lesson to be learned from the deaths of 'innocent victims' such as those haemophiliacs who contracted HIV via contaminated Factor 8 has not been yet been spelled out.

Susan Sontag in her powerful books on cancer and AIDS (1979, 1988) demonstrates the metaphors of war and combat that underlie discourses on disease. If one has cancer one faces either 'victory' or 'defeat' – to be cured or be killed. This creates the illusion of 'otherness' of the disease or disorder: the cancer could not be considered 'part of me' other than as an enemy who has infiltrated the fortress. The impact of this style of thinking on how one lives with a disease can be profound. For those who suffer from chronic disorders the 'otherness' of the disorder is difficult to identify and disentangle. How would I be, and more important to me, *who* would I be without rheumatoid arthritis? I cannot wage a war against something that is an intrinsic part of my being, personality, past and present.

THE ACCIDENT-PRONE WORKER

In the field of accident prevention, as discussed briefly in the previous chapter, there was a line of research that sought to identify that small group of workers who had the highest number of accidents. Early work considered accidents in munitions factories during the First World War. In 1919, the concept of the 'accident-prone worker' was born. A major flaw in this early work, which sought to explain differences in accident rates by considering individual differences between workers, was the assumption that all workers in a given occupational setting were exposed to the same and equal environment. This is certainly not the case; within any setting some workers, by virtue of their particular job or role in the organisation, will have different exposure to a hazard. The managing director of a brewery is much less likely to suffer a fatal accident than the worker on his factory floor.

Nevertheless, the concept of accident-proneness did not disappear. Psychologists were effective in revitalising it and focused on specific occupational groups to uncover these individual differences. Bus drivers have been shown to have different accident rates and a personality test has been designed to predict the accident behaviour of drivers (Hakkinen, 1979). The use of such tests in selection procedures carries with it dilemmas for the psychologist. On the one hand, it could be argued that it is vitally important to select the safest possible bus drivers or airline pilots since the lives of so many people are in their hands. But the other side of the argument is that we need to be very certain that the personality make-up of the individual is a critical factor in such accidents. The infrequency of accidents and the wide variation in the environmental conditions in which they occur can make conclusions drawn from the individual extremely problematic. I have heard no arguments to extend this kind of testing to other occupations, which could in theory carry an even greater risk for the unsuspecting general public. An accident-prone brain surgeon or midwife might be a far greater menace than your average bus driver. Surry (1979) has identified mediating variables in accident-proneness such as age, experience, the use of medication or drugs, motivation level and many more. Accident-proneness is unlikely to be a permanent personality characteristic and is much more likely to be related to extraneous variables such as number of hours worked, state of the roads or traffic and other dimensions. Nevertheless, after almost every major accident there is an attempt on the part of the media at least to allocate blame and identify who was at fault. A broader analysis that considered the circumstances in which the accident occurred might be more useful, but might also provide less dramatic headlines.

THE ACCIDENT-PRONE CHILD

We saw in Chapter 7 that there were marked differences in the accident rates of children. We also noted that some research had attempted to identify personality characteristics such as impulsiveness as being at the core of these differences. In 1991 in England and Wales, 185 child pedestrians were killed and nearly 4,000 received serious injuries. Roberts (1995) examined the personal characteristics of those children who were injured and compared them with those without injuries. There were no differences at all between them; but there were differences in the areas in which they lived. Children from areas with a high volume of traffic and high speed limits were at greater risk. Intervention studies aimed at teaching children safer ways to cross a road have shown improved knowledge but have failed to impact at all on behaviour and to achieve changed accident rates. Traffic calming and management schemes, on the other hand, do work. Once again the emphasis needs to be placed on public policy rather than the accident-prone individual.

BRINGING IT ON ONESELF?

Two areas directly related to preventive health where there has been evidence of discrimination on the basis of blame allocation are smoking and obesity. There have now been a number of cases reported in the press of people denied surgery because they were heavy smokers. Now I am not arguing here that the option of surgery, always risky and particularly so for those with respiratory difficulties, should not be decided on medical grounds. What is worrying though is the underlying subtext that suggests that those who have not, for whatever reason, looked after themselves cannot then expect the national health service to look after them either. Decisions about treatment are difficult, but the idea that some patients are more deserving of treatment than others is a disturbing one.

A related point concerns those who are regarded as being overweight or obese. There have been occasions when such people have also been the subject of discrimination. There is again no doubt that serious obesity can be a serious health problem, but surely this indicates more need for care and treatment, not less. Decisions to employ secretarial staff have been based on questions about their weight; there has been an instance recently where a secretary, employed on a temporary contract with a university for more than a year, and with an exemplary sickness record during that time, was informed that she could not be considered for a permanent post unless she lost weight. If we extend the argument a little further we can see the underlying prejudice that governs such decisions. Care and concern not judgement are the issues here. What about the cancer-prone personality? Or the executive who demonstrates a Type A behaviour pattern? Should we deny them employment or treatment because they have 'brought their illness upon themselves'?

The recognition that certain patterns of behaviour or styles of being may have links with disease was discussed in Chapter 4. It is a small step from that recognition to the reaction that a person who has developed cancer can't have been thinking positively, eating correctly or anything else. This increases the feelings that are naturally triggered by the news of a life-threatening condition. The more we link lifestyle to health the more we assume that our health is within our control, but the extent to which it is is limited. Almost always the major risk factors for disease are those about which we can do little: being male, being from a particular ethnic group, being born with a particular condition. We cannot all be healthy all of the time, nor should we expect to be so.

Blaming the victim also shifts responsibility away from politicians and those others such as employers who help to shape our environment. A health service with inadequate funding has to decide who to treat. Shortage of beds leads to cases being prioritised; in all circumstances some degree of this happens, but in circumstances when services are squeezed the pressure to demonstrate the deservingness of one's case grows.

SOCIAL CLASS DIFFERENCES IN HEALTH

The major role of social class in determining one's health status has often gone unacknowledged in health psychology. Inevitably psychology has as its focus the individual, but there has been perhaps too great an emphasis on personality traits predisposing to illness and too little emphasis on social aspects such as poverty as key determinants. The notable exception to this general neglect is the work of Douglas Carroll and his associates. Carroll *et al.* (1993) examine substantial variations in health which they argue are contingent on socio-economic position.

There has long been an acknowledgement that social class and mortality rates are linked. The Black Report was the outcome of the Working Group on Inequalities in Health established by the Labour Government in 1977 to examine the nature of health inequalities and to recommend corrective action. By the time it was published it was 1980 and its reception was hostile. It made depressing reading; it showed that despite more than thirty years of a national health service, there were still marked class differences in health. These differences were present at birth, with infants of manual and unskilled workers at greater risk in the first year of life than those with professional parents. Between the ages of 1 and 14 these class-based differences narrowed, but were still present. Death by accident was ten times more frequent for boys of unskilled workers than for boys of professionals. The clearest link between class and health is provided by an analysis of Standardised Mortality Ratios for different occupations. These show that the Standardised Mortality Ratio (SMR) for unskilled men in manual occupations (Social Class V) was 1.8 times that of men in professional and managerial work (Social Class I). Similar findings were reported from Australia (Taylor, 1979): SMRs for Australian males showed a ratio of 87 for professional and technical occupations compared with 152 amongst miners and quarry workers. An extremely interesting point is that these differences persisted when the SMRs of the groups are compared with respect to causes of death. Those men with manual occupations have a 65 per cent greater chance of dying from a car accident than do professional or technical workers (Russell and Schofield, 1986).

A major study on men in the Civil Service, known as the Whitehall Study, captured a group of people over a long period of time, all working in a similar environment. The risk of coronary heart disease between the various echelons of the Civil Service demonstrates the importance of class as a variable in health research.

Carroll *et al.* (1993) argue that these conventional social class indices based on occupation may even under-estimate the health differentials

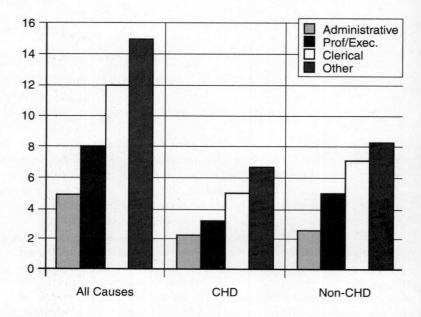

Figure 8.1 Percentage of men dying in ten years from all causes, from coronary heart disease and from non-CHD causes, by grade in the Civil Service (age-adjusted figures)

Source: Adapted, by permission from OUP, from Marmot and Mustard, 1995

that are contingent on social and material circumstances. They describe car ownership, for example, as a key indicator of health standing. Davey Smith *et al.* (1990) examined car ownership as part of the Whitehall Study of British Civil Servants. They showed that both occupational status and car ownership are independently related to mortality. The difference in mortality rate between the highest social class and being a car owner against the lowest social class without a car was 4.3. It is not being argued here that buying a car could make you healthy (unless of course it protects you from other health risks such as getting mugged whilst walking home late at night). Rather, car ownership is a clear indicator of the amount of income at one's disposal and that is, in turn, an indicator of health status.

Davey Smith *et al.* (1992) measured the height of the commemorative obelisks in Glasgow's cemeteries. Why might a health psychologist be

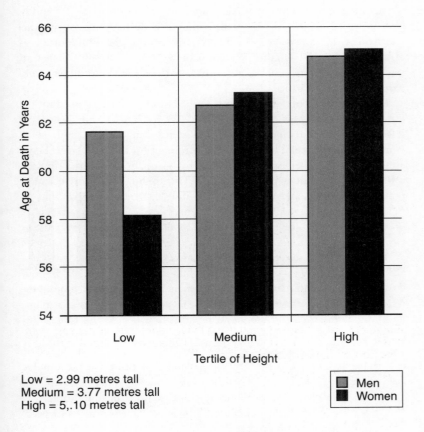

Figure 8.2 Age at death according to obelisk height in Glasgow cemeteries

Source: Carroll *et al.*, 1994

interested in doing that? Since the form of the memorial is standard, the height of it reflects the amount of money a family is willing or able to invest in such an artefact. In other words, it is an indirect measure of social standing and wealth. Davey Smith *et al.* correlated the height of obelisk with the age at death recorded on it. The resulting correlation was high, in other words, the taller the obelisk the older the person commemorated was at death. A linear regression showed that every additional metre in height of obelisk translated into an extra 1.4 years of life for men and an additional 2.2 years for women. Given that a family had to be fairly wealthy to commemorate a death in this way, this variation within a relatively small economic band is clearly important as a further indicator that the possession of wealth and assets also has an impact on how long one might expect to live even within relatively narrow social class bands.

Four categories of explanation have been put forward to account for these health differentials between social classes. They are: artefact, social selection, behaviour and lifestyle, and social causation. Carroll *et al.* consider each in turn. The basis of the argument for the differences being artefactual is that measuring social class by occupational status artificially inflates the differences between them. The findings mentioned earlier that consider assets and material wealth independently of social class do not support the argument that differences are merely an artefact of measurement techniques. If anything, such work suggests that occupational status differences in health are under-estimates.

The use of social selection as an explanation suggests that those with good health tend to move up the social scale whilst those with poor health move down. Hence, health status is taken as determining social status and not the other way around. There is obviously the possibility that long-standing health problems, such as those involving bronchitis, would affect the ability to present oneself for full-time work. The Whitehall Study, however, reported that amongst those who at the time of inclusion in the study had no discernible ill health, the mortality/social status relationship was still found to hold (Marmot *et al.*, 1984). There is some evidence of ill health during childhood as leading to a lower occupational status than might otherwise have been expected; during adulthood, however, the effect of social selection is much less likely to operate.

If differentials are not artefactual or related to social selection, then an alternative hypothesis, much favoured by government ministers, is offered. Perhaps differences in health between social groups are related to the effects of smoking, drinking and poor diet. Behavioural risk is at the heart of health psychology and much of the previous chapters was concerned with an evaluation of them. The Whitehall Study can offer us some evidence here. The social class gradients in mortality were similar if non-smokers were considered separately from smokers. Undoubtedly smoking increases mortality rate, but it was not the sole determinant of social class differences reported in this study. Similarly, there was evidence that risk of coronary heart disease was clearly related to occupational status independently of behavioural variations in physical activity, smoking, obesity and blood pressure. The Alameda County Study in the United States found that, after controlling for thirteen potential risk factors such as smoking, drinking and exercise, the gradient of mortality associated with wealth remained, with the poorest group having one and a half times greater risk than the richest group. Thus differences in risk behaviours cannot be the whole story behind status differences in health.

The fourth account considers social causation of ill health, focusing most particularly on early social circumstances. This view has received recent support from the so-called 'Barker' hypothesis. A number of studies reported since 1987 have considered the relationship between birth weight and the later development of coronary heart disease (Barker, 1991). Professor Barker and his colleagues in Southampton have formed the hypothesis that a baby's nourishment before birth and during infancy 'programmes' the development of risk factors, such as raised blood pressure, for coronary heart disease. They have studied this by considering areas of the country where measurements of infants, such as weight at birth, have been systematically collected over a long period of time. Middle-aged men have then been identified from these statistics and studied for risk of coronary heart disease. This work is controversial since a number of the factors are inferred rather than measured directly. For example, foetal nutrition is necessarily inferred from foetal growth, and birth weight might be related to later coronary heart disease not because of early nutrition, but because of its link with later body mass indices. Nevertheless, the work of Barker and others gives a good illustration of how an over-concentration on later 'lifestyle' behaviours may once again over-emphasise the amount that an individual can achieve in altering his or her risk of coronary heart disease.

Carroll *et al.* favour accounts that show that material deprivation and psychological factors such as stressful life events and lack of social support might also have a direct effect on health status. Overall, from cross-national studies it would appear that countries differ not only in their relative wealth, but also in the steepness of their social class mortality gradient. In other words, the magnitude of difference in wealth between rich and poor in a country is a key predictor of health differences. Thus both the overall wealth of the country and the steepness of the gradient would appear to be important in predicting health. Given the widening gap between rich and poor in the UK, Davey Smith and others (1990, 1992) would also predict that the difference in health status between rich and poor would also widen.

Marmot and Mustard (1995) review coronary heart disease (CHD) from a population perspective. They point out that in most western

European countries and other 'developed' countries there is now a decline in CHD mortality. This decline, however, has been concentrated among men in non-manual occupations; there has been no decline at all among men in manual occupations (Marmot and McDowell, 1986). Marmot and Mustard's work has shown that the rises and falls in CHD mortality are closely related to social and economic forces: 'the occurrence of CHD is intimately bound up with the fundamental nature of the social structures in which we live' (Marmot and Mustard (1995: 212). I suspect this is a message that will be hard to incorporate into current health promotion efforts that focus on individual lifestyles as the source of good and ill health. It is reassuring to recognise, however that at least one objective articulated in *The Health of the Nation* – that of reducing levels of ill health and death caused by CHD – is likely to be achieved – just by waiting.

The significance of this work for heath psychology and for blaming the victim is clear. Health promotion focuses on the individual changing 'risk behaviours' and adopting health behaviours to prevent ill health, yet rarely is the advice 'go out and earn more money' articulated. *The Health of the Nation* (DoH, 1992a) devotes less than a single page to what is known as 'variation' and it does not mention poverty as a cause (or even major contributor) to ill health. 'Risk' behaviours that are considered, such as smoking and drinking, do not occur in a social vacuum. Carroll *et al.* (1993, 1994) point out that a long life may be a less obvious goal if life itself is grim on a day-to-day basis. They quote a working-class respondent who asserts: 'If you don't like what you've got, you won't try and keep it very long'.

HEALTHY CITIES

Healthy Cities is an initiative from WHO linked to the move towards Health For All. The Healthy Cities Project seeks to expand the view of health into the socio-political domain. As such, it is a political programme that intends to bring about changes in the power relations associated with health and illness. It has developed out of the Ottawa Charter for Health Promotion, which defined health promotion as 'the process of enabling people to increase control over, and to improve, their health.' Healthy Cities recognises the key roles that environmental and policy decisions have on our health. Davies and Kelly quote Parfitt in this regard: 'Many would be surprised to learn that the greatest contribution to the health of the nation over the past 150 years was made, not by doctors or hospitals, but by local government' (Davies and Kelly, 1993: 17).

By 1991 WHO was working with a network of thirty project cities, most of which were in western Europe, such as Copenhagen, Glasgow, Düsseldorf and Zagreb. The aim was to develop new ideas in public health. Hunt (1993) offers a case study to illustrate some of the aspects of a healthy city project; her work can inform us here. Her chief concern was the impact of poor housing, most especially houses with damp, upon health. Up until the 1950s it was widely accepted that poor housing and ill health went together; but improvements since then have seen this element of public policy drop down health agendas. Hunt shows how the problem of housing as a hazard to health became fragmented into different domains. Allergies as a consequence of exposure to mould were the province of doctors; measuring dampness fell to environmental health officers; surveying and identifying mould was the province of micro-biologists, and housing design was the province of architects. Those who lived in such houses were not being considered effectively by any of these agencies. Hunt developed the largest study of its kind in Britain, where a tripartite study was organised that aimed to

- survey the health of children and a parent living in each dwell-ing in a specified area
- carry out a technical survey of the dwellings which included level of damp and mould and structural features
- analyse the mould taken from dwellings.

The study established that there were dose-response relationships between levels of mould in the air and the extent and type of symptoms of children in the dwellings. These findings were independent of other factors such as smoking in the households, income or household com-position. The outcome of this study was a raft of community initiatives including the gaining of money from the European Community for a solar energy demonstration project. There was also a Right to Warmth campaign, which produces booklets to inform people of the health hazards associated with damp and mouldy housing. Studies and projects such as this go some way towards ensuring the gulf between the researcher and the researched is narrowed, and the recognition that research into health is, by its very nature, a political activity.

WHO IS RESPONSIBLE?

What is being argued here is that the underlying rationale of health psychology has been to maintain personal responsibility for one's health and assumes that the individual has the wherewithal to do so: 'If a person can do much to improve health, bad health can be perceived as a personal or moral failing' (Brownell, 1991: 306).

Tesh, in a book entitled *Hidden Arguments* (1988), considers the basis of the popularity of 'lifestyle' explanations of disease. She asserts it is the cornerstone of United States health policy and suggests this is for three reasons. First, practising 'health behaviours' has come to represent individualism and upward mobility. The second reason is that it emphasises personal control over disease. Healthier living can be achieved by individual action and therefore without the need for major changes in industrial practices, environmental regulations or in government policies. Finally, if the individual can be persuaded to take responsibility for a disease, then society does not have to. Objections to imposition of social controls such as wearing seat belts or cycle helmets frequently stress the belief that social regulation shackles the expression of individuality. There is a tension between the rights of the individual to kill himself or herself and the needs of society to offer reasonable protection to that individual. Health psychology has barely considered these issues.

Similar arguments have been put forward in this country by health psychologists responding to *The Health of the Nation*. Marks (1994) described the project as having 'some fatal flaws' in that it places too heavy a reliance on human behaviour being rational, it assumes behaviour is determined independent of social and economic forces and that it is inconsistent with current research and health policy. From the point of view of this chapter, its most serious flaw is described by Marks as: 'It tends to suggest that the victims of preventable diseases are irresponsible and unworthy of protective health care' (Marks, 1994: 120). He goes on to describe the over-riding assumption of the policy that 'health is an individual responsibility' (Marks, 1994: 121). What I hope to have shown here is that choosing to ignore social, political and economic circumstances when considering preventive health is choosing to fail.

CONCLUSIONS

Many issues underlie a desire to prevent ill health and many of these issues are problematic for health psychology. The focus on the individual is natural for a sub-division of the field of Psychology; but the contents of this chapter, in combination with earlier ones, have shown that the focus needs to be broadened to include the cultural, social and, most important of all, the political dimension of health. By doing this, we may move forward in our aim to have a healthy nation.

References

Abraham, C., Sheeran, P., Adams, D., Sears, R. and Marks, D. (1991). Young people learning about AIDS: A study of beliefs and information sources. *Health Education Research: Theory and Practice*, *6*, 19–26.

Ader, R. and Cohen, N. (1985). CNS immune system interactions: Conditioning phenomena. *Behavioral and Brain Sciences*, *8*, 379–426.

Ader, R., Felton, D. L. and Cohen, N. (1991). *Psychoneuroimmunlogy*. New York: Academic Press.

Adler, N. and Matthews, K. (1994). Health psychology: Why do some people get sick and some stay well? *Annual Review of Psychology*, *45*, 229–259.

Alfred, K. D. and Smith, T. W. (1989). The hardy personality: Cognitive and physiological responses to evaluative threat. *Journal of Personality and Social Psychology*, *56*, 257–266.

Allegrante, J. P. and Sloan, R. P. (1986). Ethical dilemmas in work place health promotion. *Preventive Medicine*, *15*, 313–320.

Allen, I. (1991). *Family Planning and Counselling Projects for Young People*. London: Policy Studies Institute.

Andersen, B. L., Kiecolt-Glaser, J. K. and Glaser, R. (1994). A biobehavioral model of cancer stress and disease course. *American Psychologist*, *49*(5), 389–404.

Anderson, P. (1988). Excess mortality associated with alcohol consumption. *British Medical Journal*, *297*, 824–826.

Anderson, P., Cremona, A., Platon, A., Turner, C. and Wallace, P. (1993). The risk of alcohol. *Addiction*, *88*(11), 1493–1508.

Antoni, M. H., Schneiderman, N., Klimas, N. and LaPerriere, A. (1991). Disparities in psychological, neuroendocrine and immunologic patterns in asymptomatic HIV-1 seropositive and seronegative gay men. *Biological Psychiatry*, *29*, 1023–1041.

Antonovsky, A. (1987). *Unraveling the Mystery of Health: How People Manage Stress and Stay Well*. San Francisco: Josey-Bass.

ASH (1993). *Her Share of Misfortune*. Action on Smoking and Health.

Austoker, J. (1994a). Screening for cervical cancer. *British Medical Journal*, *309*, 241–248.

Austoker, J. (1994b). Screening for ovarian, prostate and testicular cancers. *British Medical Journal*, *309*, 315–320.

Azeem, M. F., Cook, D. G., Ross Anderson, H., Hilton, S., Bunn, S. and Stones, C. (1994). Using patient and general practice characteristics to explain variations in cervical smear uptake rates. *British Medical Journal*, *308*, 1272–1276.

Babor, T. F. and Grant, M. (1992). *WHO Collaborating Investigators Project on identification and management of alcohol-related problems. Combined analyses of outcome data: the cross-national generalizability of brief interventions. Report on phase II: A randomised clinical trial of brief interventions in primary heath care.* WHO, Copenhagen.

Baker, G. H. B. (1987). Psychological factors and immunity: Invited review. *Journal of Psychosomatic Research*, *31*(1), 1–10.

Baltimore, C. L. and Meyer, R. J. (1968). A study of storage, child behavioral traits, and mother's knowledge of toxicology in 52 poisoned families and 52 comparison families. *Pediatrics*, *42*, 312–317.

Bandura, A. (1977). *Social Learning Theory.* Englewood Cliffs, NJ: Prentice-Hall.

Bandura, A. (1986). *Social Foundations of Thought and Action: A Social Cognitive Theory.* Englewood Cliffs, NJ: Prentice-Hall.

Barker, D. J. P. (1991). The foetal and infant origins of inequalities of health in Britain. *Journal of Public Health and Medicine*, *13*, 64–68.

Bartrop, R. W., Luckhurst, E., Lazarus, L., Kiloh, L. G. and Penny, R. (1977). Depressed lymphocyte function after bereavement. *Lancet*, *1*, 834–836.

Beardow, R., Oerton, J. and Victor, C. (1989). Evaluation of the cervical cytology screening programme in an inner city health district. *British Medical Journal*, *299*, 90–100.

Becker, M. H. and Maiman, L. A. (1975). Sociobehavioral determinants of compliance with health and medical care recommendations. *Medical Care*, *13*, 10–24.

Bell, A. P. and Weinberg, M. S. (1978). *Homosexualities: A Study of Diversity among Men and Women.* New York: Simon and Schuster.

Belloc, N. B. and Breslow, L. (1972). Relationship between physical health status and health practices. *Preventive Medicine*, *1*, 409–421.

Bennet, P. and Smith, C. (1992). Parents' attitudinal and social influences on childhood vaccination. *Health Education Research: Theory and Practice*, *73*(3), 341–348.

Bennett, P., Murphy, S., Carroll, D. and Ground, I. (1995). Psychology, health promotion and aesthemiology. *Health Care Analysis*, *3*, 15–26.

Biddle, S. and Mutrie, N. (1991). *Psychology of Physical Activity: A Health Related Perspective.* London: Springer-Verlag.

Bien, T. H., Miller, W. R. and Tonigan, S. J. (1993). Brief interventions for alcohol problems: a review. *Addiction*, *88*, 315–336.

Bijur, P. E., Golding, J. and Haslum, M. (1988). Persistence of occurrence of injury: Can injuries of preschool children predict injuries of school-aged children? *Pediatrics*, *82*, 707–712.

Blair, S., Shane, N. and McKay, J. (1985). Measles matter, but do parents know? *British Medical Journal*, *290*, 623–624.

Blaxter, M. (1983). Causes of disease: women talking. *Social Science and Medicine*, *16*, 59–69.

Blue, C. L. (1995). The predictive capacity of the Theory of Reasoned Action and the Theory of Planned Behavior in exercise research – An integrated literature review. *Research in Nursing and Health*, *18*(2), 105–121.

Blum, A. and Ames, B. N. (1977). Flame retardant additives as possible cancer hazards: The main flame retardant in children's pyjamas is a mutagen and should not be used. *Science*, *195*, 17–22.

Bly, J. L., Jones, R. C. and Richardson, J. E. (1986). Impact of worksite health promotion on health care costs and utilization. *Journal of the American Medical Association*, *256*, 3235–3240.

Bobo, J. K., Gale, J. L., Thapa, P. B. and Wassilak, S. (1993). Risk factors for delayed immunization in a random sample of 1163 children from Oregon and Washington. *Pediatrics*, *91*(2), 308–314.

Bowden, F. J. (1996). Surveillance of sexually transmitted diseases in the Northern Territory of Australia. *Venereology*, *8*(1), 21–25.

Bradley, C., Brewin, C., Gamsu, D. and Moses, J. (1984). Development of scales to measure perceived control of diabetes mellitus and diabetes related health beliefs. *Diabetic Medicine*, *1*, 213–218.

Bradley, C., Lewis, K., Jennings, A. and Ward, S. (1990). Scales to measure perceived control developed specifically for people with tablet treated diabetes. *Diabetic Medicine*, *7*, 685–694.

Bradley, S. M. and Friedman, E. H. (1993). Cervical cytology screening: a comparison of uptake among 'Asian' and 'non-Asian' women in Oldham. *Journal of Public Health Medicine*, *15*(1), 46–51.

Breslow, L. and Enstrom, J. E. (1980). Persistence of health habits and their relationship to mortality. *Preventive Medicine*, *9*, 469–483.

Broadbent, D. E., Broadbent, M. H. P., Phillpotts, R. J. and Wallace, J. (1984). Some further studies of the prediction of experimental colds in volunteers by psychological factors. *Journal of Psychosomatic Research*, *28*(6), 511–523.

Brownell, K. D. (1991). Personal responsibility and control over our bodies: When expectation exceeds reality. *Health Psychology*, *10*(5), 303–310.

Brubaker, R. and Fowler, C. (1990). Encouraging college males to perform testicular self examination: Evaluation of a persuasive message based on the revised Theory of Reasoned Action. *Journal of Applied Social Psychology*, *17*, 1411–1422.

Brubaker, R. G. and Wickersham, D. (1990). Encouraging the practice of testicular self examination: A field application of the Theory of Reasoned Action. *Health Psychology*, *9*(2), 154–163.

Caceres, C. F., Rosasco, A. M., Mandel, J. S. and Hearst, N. (1994). Evaluating a school-based intervention for STD/AIDS prevention in Peru. *Journal of Adolescent Health*, *15*(7), 582–591.

Calle, E. E., Flanders, W. D., Thun, M. J. and Martin, L. M. (1993). Demographic predictors of mammography and pap smear screening in U.S. women. *American Journal of Public Health*, *83*(1), 53–60.

Calnan, M. (1984). The health belief model and participation in programmes for the early detection of cancer: A comparative analysis. *Social Science and Medicine*, *19*(8), 823–830.

Calnan, M. (1987). *Health and Illness: The Lay Perspective*. London: Tavistock.

Calnan, M. and Rutter, D. R. (1986). Do health beliefs predict health behaviour? *Social Science and Medicine*, *22*(6), 673–678.

Calnan, M. and Rutter, D. R. (1988). Do health beliefs predict health behaviour? A follow up analysis of breast self examination. *Social Science and Medicine*, *26*(4), 463–465.

Cameron, M. H., Vulcan, A. P., Finch, C. F. and Newstead, S. V. (1994). Mandatory bicycle helmet use following a decade of helmet promotion in Victoria, Australia – An evaluation. *Accident Analysis and Prevention*, *26*(3), 325–337.

Cardenas, M. P. and Simons-Morton, B. G. (1993). The effect of anticipatory guidance on mothers' self-efficacy and behavioral intentions to prevent burns caused by hot tap water. *Patient Education and Counselling*, *21*, 117–123.

Carrol, D. and Cross, G. (1990). The academics who double as electricians. *The Independent*, 23 October: 23.

Carroll, D., Bennett, P. and Smith, G. D. (1993). Socio-economic health inequalities – Their origins and implications. *Psychology and Health*, *8*(5), 295–316.

Carroll, D., Davey Smith, G. and Bennett, P. (1994). Health and socio-economic status. *The Psychologist*, *7*(3), 122–125.

Carver, C. S., Scheier, M. F. and Weintraub, J. K. (1989). Assessing coping strategies: a theoretically based approach. *Journal of Personality and Social Psychology*, *56*(2), 267–283.

Cassileth, B. R., Lusk, E. J., Miller, D. S., Brown, L. L. and Miller, C. (1985). Psychosocial correlates of survival in advanced malignant diseases. *New England Journal of Medicine*, *312*, 1551–1555.

Champion, V. L. (1993). Instrument refinement for breast cancer screening behaviors. *Nursing Research*, *42*(3), 139–143.

Champion, V. L. (1994). Strategies to increase mammography utilization. *Med Care*, *32*(2), 118–129.

Champion, V. L. and Scott, C. (1993). Effects of a procedural/belief intervention on breast self examination performance. *Research in Nursing and Health*, *16*, 163–170.

Chapman, S., Wong, W. L. and Smith, W. (1993). Self exempting beliefs about smoking and health: Differences between smokers and ex-smokers. *American Journal of Public Health*, *83*(2), 215–219.

Coates, T. J. (1989). Behavioral co-factors and AIDS progression. At *Society of Behavioral Medicine*, San Francisco, CA.

Cody, R. and Lee, C. (1990). Behaviours, beliefs, and intentions in skin cancer protection. *Journal of Behavioral Medicine*, *13*, 373–389.

Cohen, S., Tyrrell, D. A. J. and Smith, A. P. (1991). Psychological stress and susceptibility to the common cold. *New England Journal of Medicine*, *325*, 606–612.

Cohen, S., Tyrrell, D. A. J. and Smith, A. P. (1993). Negative life events, perceived stress, negative affect, and susceptibility to the common cold. *Journal of Personality and Social Psychology*, *64*(1), 131–140.

Cohen, W. S. (1985). Health promotion in the workplace. *American Psychologist*, *40*(2), 213–216.

Cooper, C. L. (1986). *Stress and Breast Cancer*. Chichester: John Wiley & Sons.

Cooper, C. L. and Williams, S. (1994). Conclusions to creating healthy work organizations. In C. L. Cooper and S. Williams (Eds) *Creating Healthy Work Organizations* (pp. 243–246). Chichester: John Wiley & Sons.

Cooper, C. L., Cooper, R. D. and Faragher, B. (1986). Psychosocial stress as a precursor to breast cancer: A review. *Current Psychological Research and Reviews*, *5*(3), 268–280.

Cooper, P., Diamond, I. and High, S. (1992). *Choosing and Using Contraceptives: Consumers' Experience in Wessex. Opportunities and Choice: Quality Measures in Family Planning Services.* Southampton: University of Southampton.

Craun, A. and Deffenbacher, J. (1987). The effects of information, behavior rehearsal, and prompting on breast self exams. *Journal of Behavioral Medicine*, *10*(4), 351–365.

Crews, D. J. and Landers, D. M. (1987). A meta-analytic review of aerobic fitness and reactivity to psychological stressors. *Medicine and Science in Sports and Exercise*, *19* (5, Supplement), S115–120.

Croyle, R. T. and Barger, S. D. (1993). Illness cognition. In S. Maes, H. Leventhal and M. Johnston (Eds) *International Review of Health Psychology* (pp. 29–52). Chichester: John Wiley & Sons.

Dalphinis, J. (1986). Do immunisation defaulters know enough about immunisation? *Health Visitor*, *59*, 342–344.

Dannenberg, A. and Vernick, J. (1993). A proposal for the mandatory inclusion of helmets with new children's bicycles. *American Journal of Public Health*, *83*(5), 644–646.

Dannenberg, A., Cote, T., Kresnow, M., Sack, J., Lipstiz, C. and Schmidt, E. (1993a). Bicycle helmet use by adults: The impact of companionship. *Public Health Reports*, *108*(2), 215.

Dannenberg, A., Bielson, P., Wilson, M. and Joffe, A. (1993b). Bicycle helmet laws and educational campaigns: An evaluation of strategies to increase children's helmet use. *American Journal of Public Health*, *83*(5), 667–673.

Davey Smith, G., Carroll, D., Rankin, S. and Rowan, D. (1992). Socioeconomic differentials in mortality: Evidence from Glasgow graveyards. *British Medical Journal*, *305*, 1554–1557.

Davey Smith, G., Shipley, M. J. and Rose, G. (1990). The magnitude and causes of socioeconomic differentials in mortality: Further evidence from the Whitehall study. *Journal of Epidemiology and Community Health*, *44*, 265–270.

Davies, J. K. and Kelly, M. P. (1993). *Health Cities: Research and Practice.* London: Routledge.

DiClemente and Temoshok (1985).

Dishman, R. K. (1991). Increasing and maintaining exercise and physical activity. *Behavior Therapy*, *22*, 345–378.

DoH (1992a). *The Health of the Nation.* London: HMSO.

DoH (1992b). *Immunisation against Infectious Disease.* London: HMSO.

DoH (1993). *Mortality Statistics.* Office of Population Census and Survey. London: HMSO.

Downing, C. (1993). Knowledge and risk perception: maternity staff awareness of viral hepatitis B infection. *Proceedings of the Annual Conference of the BPS Special Group in Health Psychology*, at Nottingham University.

Eadie, A. G. (1991). Moderate consumption of alcohol is beneficial to health. *British Journal of Addiction*, *86*, 380–381.

Edwards, V. (1980). Changing breast self examination behaviour. *Nursing Research*, *29*, 301–306.

Eichelberger, M. R., Gotschall, C. S., Feely, H. B., Harstad, P. and Bowman, L. M. (1990). Parental attitudes and knowledge of child safety. *American Journal of Diseases of Children*, *144*, 714–720.

Eiser, J. R., Eiser, C. and Pauwels, P. (1993). Skin cancer: Assessing perceived risk and behavioural attitudes. *Psychology and Health*, *8*, 393–404.

Elliot, E., Pitts, M. and McMaster, J. (1992). Nurses' views of parasuicide in a developing country. *International Journal of Social Psychiatry*, *38*(4), 273–279.

Evans, P. D. and Edgerton, N. (1992). Life events and mood as predictors of the common cold. *Journal of Medical Psychology*, *64*, 35–44.

Evans, P. D. and Pitts, M. K. (1994). Vulnerability to respiratory infection and the four day desirability dip: Comments on Stone, Porter and Neale. *Journal of Medical Psychology*, *67*, 387–389.

Evans, P. D., Pitts, M. K. and Smith, K. (1988). Minor infections, minor life events and the four day desirability dip. *Journal of Psychosomatic Research*, *32*, 533–539.

Fallowfield, L. (1991). *Breast Cancer*. London: Routledge.

Fallowfield, L., Rodway, A. and Baum, A. (1990). What are the psychological factors influencing attendance, non-attendance and re-attendance at a breast screening centre? *Journal of the Royal Society of Medicine*, *83*, 547–551.

Fielding, J. E. (1979). Preventive medicine and the bottom line. *Journal of Occupational Medicine*, *21*(2), 79–88.

Fielding, J. E. (1991). The challenges of work-place health promotions. In S. M. Weiss, J. E. Fielding and A. Baum (Eds) *Health at Work* (pp. 13–28). Hillsdale, New Jersey: Lawrence Erlbaum Associates.

Finney, J. W. (1995). Editorial: Pediatric injury control – Adding pieces to the puzzle. *Journal of Pediatric Psychology*, *20*(1), 1–3.

Finney, J. W., Christopherson, E.R., Friman, P. C., Kalnins, I. V., Maddux, J. E., Peterson, L., Roberts, M. C. and Wolraich, M. (1993). Society of Pediatric Psychology task force report: Pediatric psychology and injury control. *Journal of Pediatric Psychology*, *18*(4), 499–526.

Fischoff, B., Bostrum, A. and Quadrel, M. J. (1993). Risk perception and communication. *Annual Review of Public Health*, *14*, 183–203.

Fishbein, M. (1993). Introduction. In D. J. Terry, C. Gallois and M. McCamish (Eds) *The Theory of Reasoned Action: Its Application to AIDS-Preventive Behaviour*. Oxford: Pergamon Press.

Fletcher, R. (1994). Prostate cancer screening and men's health. *Australian Journal of Public Health*, *18*(4), 449–451.

Fletcher, S., Morgan, T., M'Malley, M., Earp, J. A. and Degnan, D. (1989). Is breast self examination predicted by knowledge, attitudes, beliefs of socio-demographic characteristics. *American Journal of Preventive Medicine*, *5*(4), 207–215.

Ford, C. S. and Beach, F. A. (1952). *Patterns of Sexual Behaviour*. London: Methuen.

Foster, R. S., Lang, S. P., Constanza, M. C., Worden, J. K., Haines, C. R. and Yates, J. W. (1978). Breast self examination practice and breast cancer stage. *New England Journal of Medicine*, *229*, 265–270.

Foulds, J. (1993). Editorial: Does nicotine replacement therapy work? *Addiction*, *88*, 1473–1478.

Freed, G. L., Bordley, C. W. and Defries, G. H. (1993). Childhood immunisation programs: An analysis of policy issues. *The Milbank Quarterly*, *71*(1), 65–96.

Friedman, H. S., Tucker, J. S., Schqartz, J. E., Tomlinson-Keasey, C., Martin, L. R., Wingard, D. L. and Criqui, M. H. (1995). Psychosocial and behavioral predictors of longevity. *American Psychologist*, *50*(2), 69–78.

Froines, J. and Baker, D. (1985). Workers. In R. D. W. Holland and G. Knox (Eds) *Oxford Textbook of Public Health, Vol. 4.* New York: Oxford University Press.

Funk, S. C. and Houston, B. K. (1987). A critical analysis of the Hardiness Scale's validity and utility. *Journal of Personality and Social Psychology, 53,* 572–578.

Furnham, A. F. (1988). *Lay Theories: Everyday Understanding of Problems in the Social Sciences.* Oxford: Pergamon Press.

Furnham, A. and Steele, H. (1993). Measuring locus of control: A critique of general, children's health- and work-related locus of control questionnaires. *British Journal of Psychology, 84*(4), 443–480.

Ganellen, R. J. and Blaney, P. H. (1984). Hardiness and social support as moderators of the effects of life stress. *Journal of Personality and Social Psychology* (47, 156–163.

Gene, J., Espinola, A., Cabezas, C., Boix, C., Comin, E., Martin, A. and Sanz, E. (1992). Do knowledge and attitudes about influenza and its immunization affect the likelihood of obtaining immunization? *Family Practice Research Journal, 12*(1), 61–73.

Geyer, S. (1993). Life events, chronic difficulties and vulnerability factors preceding breast cancer. *Social Science and Medicine, 37*(12), 1545–1555.

Geyer, S., Broer, M., Haltenhof, H., Buhler, K. E. and Merschbacher, U. (1994). The evaluation of life event data. *Journal of Psychosomatic Research, 38*(8), 823–835.

Glaser, R., Pearson, G. R., Bonneau, R. H., Esterling, B. A., Atkinson, C. and Kiecolt-Glaser, J. K. (1993). Stress and the memory T-cell response to the Epstein-Barr virus in healthy medical students. *Health Psychology, 12*(6), 435–442.

Glik, D., Kronenfeld, J. and Jackson, K. (1991). Predictors of risk perceptions of childhood injury among parents of preschoolers. *Health Education Quarterly, 18,* 285–301.

Goddard, E. (1992). Why children start smoking. *British Journal of Addiction, 87,* 17–25.

Gorczynski, R. M., Macrae, S. and Kennedy, M. (1982). Conditioned immune response associated with allogenei skin grafts in mice. *Journal of Immunology, 129,* 704–709.

Gould-Martin, K., Paganini-Hill, A., Casagrande, C., Mack, T. and Ross, R. K. (1982). Behavioral and biological determinants of surgical stage of breast cancer. *Preventive Medicine, 11,* 429–440.

Graham, H. (1993). *Women, Smoking and Low Income.*

Graitcer, P. L. and Sniezek, J. L. (1988). Hospitalizations due to tap water scalds 1978–1985. *MMWR-CDC-Surveillance Summa;ry, 37*(Feb), 35–38.

Gray-Toft, P. and Anderson, J. G. (1991). The nursing stress scale: Development of an instrument. *Journal of Behavioral Assessment, 3,* 11–23.

Greer, S. and Morris, T. (1975). Psychological attributes of women who develop breast cancer: A controlled study. *Journal of Psychosomatic Research, 19,* 147–153.

Greer, S., Morris, T. and Pettingale, K. W. (1979). Psychological response to breast cancer: effect on outcome. *Lancet, ii,* 785–787.

Ground, I. (1995). Psychology, health promotion and aesthemiology. 2. What you do is determined by what you do. *Health Care Analysis, 3*(1), 22–26.

Gruman, J. and Sloan, R. (1983). Disease as justice: Perceptions of the victims of physical illness. *Basic and Applied Social Psychology*, *4*, 49–56.

Hakkinen, S. (1979). Traffic accidents and professional driver characteristics: a follow up study. *Accident Analysis and Prevention*, *58*, 1431–1438.

Hallal, J. (1982). The relationship of health beliefs, health locus of control, and self concept to the practice of breast self examination in adult women. *Nursing Research*, *31*(3), 137–142.

Harris, K. B. and Miller, W. R. (1990). Behavioral self control training for problem drinkers: Components of efficacy. *Psychology of Addictive Behaviors*, *4*, 82–90.

Harrison, J. A., Mullen, P. D. and Green, L. (1992). A meta-analysis of studies of the health education model with adults. *Health Education Research*, 7, 107–116.

Hennig, P. and Knowles, A. (1990). Factors influencing women over 40 years to take precautions against cervical cancer. *Journal of Applied Social Psychology*, *20*(19), 1612–1621.

Hennrikus, D., Girgia, A., Redman, S. and Sanson-Fisher, R. W. (1991). A community study of delay in presenting to medical practitioners with signs of melanoma. *Archives of Dermatology*, *127*, 356–361.

Herbert, & Cohen (1993a). Depression and immunity. *Psychological Bulletin*, *113*(3), 472–486.

Herbert, & Cohen (1993b). Stress and immunity in humans: A meta analytic review. *Psychosomatic Medicine*, *55*, 364–379.

Hewitt, M. (1989). The incidence of contraindications. *Archives of Disease in Childhood*, *64*(7), 1052–1053.

Hill, D. and Shugg, D. (1989). Breast self examination practices and attitudes among breast cancer, benign breast disease and general practice patients. *Health Education Research*, *4*(2), 193–203.

Hill, D., Gardner, G. and Rassaby, J. (1985). Factors predisposing women to take precautions against breast and cervical cancer. *Journal of Applied Social Psychology*, *15*(1), 59–79.

Hill, D., White, V., Jolley, D. and Mapperson, K. (1988). Self examination of the breast: Is it beneficial? Meta-analysis of studies investigating breast self examination and extent of disease in patients with breast cancer. *British Medical Journal*, *297*(23 July), 271–275.

Hobbs, P., Haran, D., Pendleton, L. L., Jones, B. E. and Posner, T. (1984). Public attitudes and cancer education. *International Review of Applied Psychology*, *33*, 565–586.

Holmes, K. K. and Aral, S. O. (1991). Behavioural interventions in developing countries. In J. N. Wasserheit, S. O. Aral and K. K. Holmes (Eds) *Research Issues in Human Behaviour and Sexually Transmitted Diseases in the AIDS Era*. Washington D.C.: American Society for Microbiology.

Howard, J. (1993). Improving accident prevention for older people. *Journal of the Royal Society of Health*, 266–268.

Hunt, S. M. (1993). The relationship between research and policy. In J. K. Davies and M. P. Kelly (Eds) *Health Cities: Research and Practice*. London: Routledge.

Jackson, H. (1992). *AIDS: Action Now: Information, prevention and support in Zimbabwe*. Harare: AIDS Counselling Trust.

Jackson, H. and Pitts, M. K. (1991). Company policy on AIDS in Zimbabwe. *Journal of Social Development in Africa*, 6(2), 53–70.

Janis, I. L. and Mann, I. (1977). *Decision Making: A Psychological Analysis of Conflict, Choice and Commitment*. New York: Free Press.

Janz, N. K. and Becker, M. H. (1984). The Health Belief Model: A decade later. *Health Education Quarterly*, 11, 1–47.

Jaquess, D. L. and Finney, J. W. (1994). Previous injuries and behavior problems predict children's injuries. *Journal of Pediatric Psychology*, 19(1), 79–89.

Jarvis, M. J. (1994). A profile of tobacco smoking. *Addiction*, 89, 1371–1376.

Jenkins, C. D. (1966). Group differences in perception: A study of community beliefs and feelings about tuberculosis. *American Journal of Sociology*, 7, 471–429.

Jepsom, C. and Rimer, B. K. (1993). Determinants of mammography intentions among prior screenees and nonscreenees. *Journal of Applied Social Psychology*, 23(1), 40–51.

Johnson, A. M. and Wadsworth, J. (1994a). Heterosexual partnerships. In K. Wellings, J. Field, A. M. Johnson and J. Wadsworth (Eds) *Sexual Behaviour in Britain*. London: Penguin.

Johnson, A. M. and Wadsworth, J. (1994b). Heterosexual practices. In K. Wellings, J. Field, A. M. Johnson and J. Wadsworth (Eds) *Sexual Behaviour in Britain*. London: Penguin.

Johnson, A. M., Wadsworth, J. and Elliott, P. (1989). A pilot study of sexual lifestyle in a random sample of the population of Great Britain. *AIDS*, 3, 135–141.

Johnson, A. M., Wadsworth, J., Field, J., Wellings, K. and Anderson, R. M. (1990). Surveying sexual lifestyles. *Nature*, 343, 109.

Johnson, A. M., Wadsworth, J., Wellings, K., Bradshaw, S. and Field, J. (1992). Sexual behaviour and HIV risk. *Nature*, 360, 410–412.

Karasek, R. A. (1979). Job demands, job decision latitude and mental strain: Implications for job redesign. *Administrative Science Quarterly*, 24, 285–308.

Keane, V., Stanton, B., Horton, L., Aronson, R., Galbraith, J. and Hughart, N. (1993). Perceptions of vaccine efficiency, illness and health among inner city parents. *Clinical Pediatrics*, 32(1), 2–7.

Kemeny, M. E. (1991). Psychological factors, immune processes, and the course of herpes simplex and human immunodeficiency virus infection. In N. Plotnikoff, A. Murgo, R. Faith and J. Wybran (Eds) *Stress and Immunity* (pp. 199–210). Boca Raton, FL: CRC Press.

Kemeny, M. E., Weiner, H., Taylor, S. E., Schneider, S., Visscher, B. and Fahey, J. L. (1994). Repeated bereavement, depressed mood, and immune parameters in HIV seropositive and seronegative gay men. *Health Psychology*, 13(1), 14–24.

Kendrick, D., West, J., Wright, S. and Presbury, M. (1995). Does routine child health surveillance reach children most at risk of accidental injury? *Journal of Public Health Medicine*, 17(1), 39–45.

Kessler, R. C., Foster, C., Joseph, J., Ostrow, D., Wortman, C., Phair, J. and Chmiel, J. (1991). Stressful life events and symptom onset in HIV infection. *American Journal of Psychiatry*, 148, 733–738.

Kidd, J., Cook, R. and Marteau, T. M. (1993). Is routine AFP screening in pregnancy reassuring? *Journal of Psychosomatic Research*, 37(7), 717–722.

Kiecolt-Glaser, J. K. and Glaser, R. (1988). Psychological influences on immunity: Implications for AIDS. *American Psychologist*, 43, 892–898.

Kiecolt-Glaser, J. K., Garner, W., Speicher, C. E., Penn, G. and Glaser, R. (1984). Psychosocial modifiers of immunocompetence in medical students. *Psychosomatic Medicine*, 46, 7–14.

Kiecolt-Glaser, J. M., Fisher, L., Ogrocki, P., Stout, J. C., Speicher, C. E. and Glaser, R. (1987). Marital quality, marital disruption, and immune function. *Psychosomatic Medicine*, 49, 13–34.

Kiecolt-Glaser, J. K., Malarkey, W. B., Chee, M. A., Newton, T., Cacioppo, J. T., Mao, H. Y. and Glaser, R. (1993). Negative behavior during marital conflict is associated with immunological down-regulation. *Psychosomatic Medicine*, 55, 395–409.

Kinlay, S. and Heller, R. F. (1990). Effectiveness and hazards of case finding for a high cholesterol concentration. *British Medical Journal*, 300, 1545–1547.

Kinnersley, P. (1990). Attitudes of general practitioners towards their vaccination against Hepatitis B. *British Medical Journal*, 300(6719), 238.

Kinsey, A. C., Pomeroy, W. B. and Martin, C. E. (1948). *Sexual Behavior in the Human Male*. Philadelphia: Saunders.

Kinsey, A. C., Pomeroy, W. B., Martin, C. E. and Gebhard, P. H. (1953). *Sexual Behavior in the Human Female*. Philadelphia: Saunders.

Kivilan, D. R., Coppel, D. B., Fromme, K., Williams, E. and Marlatt, G. A. (1989). Secondary prevention of alcohol-related problems in young adults at risk. In K. D. Craig and S. M. Weiss (Eds) *Prevention and Early Intervention: Biobehavioural Perspectives*. New York: Springer.

Klein, N., Morgan, K. and Wansbrough-Jones, M. H. (1989). Parents' beliefs about vaccination: The continuing propagation of false contraindications. *British Medical Journal*, 298(6689), 1687–1688.

Knox, E. G., MacArthur, C. and Simons, K. J. (1993). *Sexual Behaviour and AIDS in Britain*. London: HMSO.

Kobasa, S. C. (1979). Stressful life events and health: An enquiry into hardiness. *Journal of Personality and Social Psychology*, 37, 1–11.

Kobasa, S. C., Maddi, S. R., Puccetti, M. C. and Zola, M. A. (1985). Effects of hardiness, exercise and social support as resources against illness. *Journal of Psychosomatic Research*, 29, 525–533.

Kramer, L. (1993). *The Normal Heart*. London: N. Hern Assoc.

Laidman, P. (1987). *Health Visiting and Preventing Accidents to Children (No. 12)*. London: Child Accident Prevention Trust.

Laitinen, H. and Vahapassi, A. (1992). Accidents at work. In J. Jeyaratnam (Ed.) *Occupational Health in Developing Countries*. Oxford: Oxford University Press.

Lam, L., Sze, P. C., Sacks, H. S. and Chalmers, T. C. (1987). Meta-analysis of randomised controlled trials of nicotine chewing gum. *Lancet*, ii, 27–29.

Landman, P. E. and Landman, G. B. (1987). Accidental injuries in children in day-care centers. *American Journal of Diseases in Children*, 141, 292–293.

Langley, J. and Silva, P. A. (1982). Childhood accidents: parents' attitudes to prevention. *Australian Pediatric Journal*, 18, 247–249.

Langley, J. D., McGee, R., Silva, P. A. and Williams, S. (1983). Child behavior and accidents. *Journal of Pediatric Psychology*, 8, 181–189.

Leakey, P., Littlewood, M., Reynolds, S. and Bunce, D. (1994). Caring for the carers: North Derbyshire Health Authority. In C. L. Cooper and S. Williams

(Eds) *Creating Healthy Work Organisations* (pp. 167–196). Chichester: John Wiley & Sons.

Ledermann, S. (1964). *Alcool, alcoolisme, alcoolisation. Mortalité, morbidité, accidents du travail.* Paris: Presses Universitaires de France.

Ledermann, S. (1965). *Alcool, alcoolisme, alcoolisation. Vol. 1.* Paris: Presses Universitaires de France.

Lee, S. H., Ewert, D. P. and Frederick, P. D. (1992). Resurgence of congenital rubella syndrome in the 1990s. *Journal of the American Medical Association, 267,* 1942–1946.

Leventhal, H. and Cameron, L. (1987). Behavioral theories and the problem of compliance. *Patient Education and Counselling, 10,* 117–138.

Lindholm, L. H., Ekbom, T., Dash, C., Eriksson, M., Tibblin, G. and Schersten, B. (1995). The impact of health care advice in primary care on cardiovascular risk. *British Medical Journal, 310,* 1105–1109.

Linn, M. W., Linn, B. S. and Stein, S. R. (1982). Beliefs about causes of cancer in cancer patients. *Social Science and Medicine, 17,* 59.

Lochhead, Y. J. (1991). Failure to immunize children under the age of 5 years: A literature review. *Journal of Advanced Nursing, 16*(2), 130–137.

Longnecker, M. P. and MacMahon, B. (1988). A meta-analysis of alcohol consumption in relation to risk of breast cancer. *Journal of the American Medical Association, 260,* 652–656.

Lowe, C. S. and Radius, S. M. (1987). Young adults' contraceptive practices: An investigation of influences. *Adolescence, 22,* 291–304.

McCarthy, W. H. and Shaw, H. M. (1989). Skin cancer in Australia. *The Medical Journal of Australia, 150,* 469–470.

McCaul, K. D., Sandgren, A. K., O'Neill, H. K. and Hinsz, V. B. (1993). The value of the theory of planned behavior, perceived control, and self efficacy expectations for predicting health-protective behaviors. *Basic and Applied Social Psychology, 14*(2), 231–252.

McCusker, J. and Morrow, G. R. (1977). The relationship of health locus of control to preventive health behaviors and health beliefs. *Patient Education and Health Counselling, 1,* 146–150.

McGee, R., Williams, S. and Elwood, M. (1994). Depression and the development of cancer – A meta-analysis. *Social Science and Medicine, 38*(1), 187–192.

McKie, L. (1993). Women's views of the cervical smear test: implications for nursing practice – women who have not had a smear test. *Journal of Advanced Nursing, 18,* 972–979.

McMaster, J., Pitts, M. and Wilson, P. (1994). The practice of testicular self examination: A comparative study of British and Zimbabwean undergraduates. *Central African Journal of Medicine, 40*(6), 154–158.

Mahoney, C. A., Thombs, D. L. and Ford, O. J. (1995). Health belief and self-efficacy models: Their utility in explaining college student condom use. *AIDS Education and Prevention, 7*(1), 32–49.

Marks, D. (1994). Psychology's role in *The Health of the Nation. The Psychologist, 7*(3), 119–121.

Marlatt, G. A. and George, W. H. (1988). Relapse prevention and the maintenance of optimal health. In S. Shumaker, E. Schron and O. S. Ockene (Eds) *The Adoption and Maintenance of Behaviors for Optimal Health.* New York: Brunner/Mazel.

Marmot, M. and Bruner, E. (1991). Alcohol and cardiovascular disease: The status of the U shaped curve. *British Medical Journal, 303*, 565–568.

Marmot, M. G. and McDowell, M. E. (1986). Mortality decline and widening social inequalities. *Lancet, ii*, 274–276.

Marmot, M. G. and Mustard, J. F. (1994). Coronary heart disease from a population perspective. In R. G. Evans, M. L. Barer and T. R. Marmor (Eds) *Why Are Some People Healthy and Others Not?* (pp. 189–192) Hawthorne, NY: Walter de Gruyter Inc.

Marmot, M. G., Shipley, M. J. and Rose, G. (1984). Inequalities in health: specific explanations of a general pattern? *Lancet, i*, 431–438.

Marteau, T. (1993). Health-related screening: psychological predictors of uptake and impact. In S. Maes, H. Leventhal and M. Johnston (Eds) *International Review of Health Psychology*. London: John Wiley & Sons.

Marteau, T. M. and Drake, H. (1995). Attributions for disability: The influence of genetic screening. *Social Science and Medicine, 40*(8), 1127–1132.

Marteau, T. and Johnston, M. (1990). Health professionals: A source of variance in patient outcomes. *Health Psychology, 5*, 47–58.

Marteau, T., Kidd, J., Cook, R., Johnston, M., Michie, S., Shaw, R. and Slack, J. (1988). Screening for Down's syndrome. *British Medical Journal, 297*, 1469.

Marteau, T., Johnston, M., Kidd, J., Michie, S., Cook, R., Slack, J. and Shaw, R. (1992). Psychological models in predicting uptake of prenatal screening. *Psychology and Health, 6*, 13–22.

Marteau, T., Kidd., J., Michie, S., Cook, R., Johnston, M. and Shaw, R. W. (1993). Anxiety, knowledge and satisfaction in women receiving false positive results on routine prenatal screening: A randomized controlled trial. *Journal of Psychosomatic and Obstetric Gynaecology, 14*, 185–196.

Masters, W. H. and Johnson, V. E. (1966). *Human Sexual Response*. Boston: Little, Brown.

Masters, W. H. and Johnson, V. E. (1970). *Human Sexual Inadequacy*. Boston: Little, Brown.

Meadows, P. (1987). Study of the women overdue for a smear test in a general practice cervical screening programme. *Journal of the Royal College of General Practitioners, 37*, 500–503.

Mellanby, A., Phelps, F., Lawrence, C. and Tripp, J. H. (1992). Teenagers and the risk of sexually transmitted diseases: A need for the provision of balanced information. *Genitourinary Medicine, 68*, 241–244.

Michie, S., Johnston, M., Cockcroft, A., Ellinghouse, C. and Gooch, C. (1995). Methods and impact of health screening for hospital staff. *Journal of Organizational Behavior, 16*(1), 85–92.

Miller, W. R. and Sanchez, V. C. (1993). Motivating young adults for treatment and lifestyle changes. In T. Loberg, W. R. Miller, P. E. Nathan and G. A. Marlatt (Eds) *Addictive Behaviors: Prevention and Early Intervention* (pp. 219–311). Amsterdam: Swets and Zeitlinger.

Mitchell, M. (1985). Disadvantaged children. *Community Outlook, 27*.

Moore, S. and Rosenthal, D. (1993). *Sexuality in Adolescence*. London: Routledge.

Moore, S. M., Rosenthal, D. A. and Boldero, J. (1993). Predicting AIDS-preventive behaviour among adolescents. In D. J. Terry, C. Gallois and M. McCamish (Eds) *The Theory of Reasoned Action: Its Application to AIDS-preventive Behaviour* (pp. 1–29). Oxford: Pergamon Press.

Moses, S., Muia, E., Bradley, J. E., Nagelkerke, N. J. D., Ngugi, E. N., Njeru, E. K., Eldridge, G., Olenja, J., Wotton, K., Plummer, F. A. and Brunham, R. C. (1994a). Sexual behaviour in Kenya – Implications for sexually transmitted disease tramsmission and control. *Social Science and Medicine*, *39*(12), 1649–1656.

Moses, S., Ngugi, E. N., Bradley, J. E., Njeru, E. K., Eldridge, G., Muia, E., Olenja, J. and Plummer, F. A. (1994b). Health care-seeking behavior related to the transmission of sexually transmitted diseases in Kenya. *American Journal of Public Health*, *84*(12), 1947–1951.

Nathoo, V. (1988). Investigation of non-responders at a cervical screening clinic in Manchester. *British Medical Journal*, *296*, 1041–1042.

Neef, N., Scutchfield, D., Elder, J. and Bender, S. (1991). Testicular self examination by young men: An analysis of characteristics associated with practice. *Journal of American College Health*, *39*(4), 187–190.

New, S. J. and Senior, M. L. (1991). I don't believe in needles; qualitative aspects of study into the uptake of infant immunisation in two English health authorities. *Social Science and Medicine*, *33*(4), 509–518.

Ng, T. P. (1992). Occupational lung diseases – mineral dusts. In J. Jeyaratnam (Ed) *Occupational Health in Developing Countries*. Oxford: Oxford University Press.

Ngugi, E. (1988). Durability of changed sexual behaviour in Nairobi prostitutes: Increasing use of condoms. In *Third International Conference on AIDS and Associated Cancers in Africa*. Arusha, Tanzania, 14–16 September.

Nichol, A. and Ross, E. (1985). Immunisation: Reducing the uncertainty. *Health Visitor*, *58*, 285.

Nichols, S. (1983). The Southampton Breast Study – Implications for nurses. *Nursing Times* (14 December), 24–27.

Nilssen, O. and Cone, H. (1994). Screening patients for alcohol problems in primary health care settings. *Alcohol and Health Research World*, *18*(2), 136–139.

Norman, P. (1993). Predicting the uptake of health checks in general practice: Invitation methods and patients' health beliefs. *Social Science and Medicine*, *37*(1), 53–59.

Norman, P. and Conner, M. (1993). The role of social cognition models in predicting attendance at health checks. *Psychology and Health*, *8*(6), 447–462.

Norman, P. and Fitter, M. (1991). Patients' views on health screening in general practice. *Family Practice*, *8*(2), 129–132.

O'Connor, P. J. 91982). Poisoning prevention: results of a public media campaign. *Australian Pediatric Journal*, *18*, 250–252.

Oakley, A., Fullerton, D., Holland, J., Arnold, S., France-Dawson, M., Kelley, P. and McGrellis, S. (1995). Sexual health education interventions for young people: a methodological review. *British Medical Journal*, *310*, 158–162.

Oborne, D. (1982). *Ergonomics at Work*. Norwich: John Wiley & Sons.

Ogden, J. and Harden, A. (1995). Beliefs about condoms in 12/13 and 16/17 year olds. *AIDS Care*, *7*(2), 205–210.

Orbell, S. and Sheeran, P. (1993). Health psychology and uptake of preventive health services – A review of 30 years' research on cervical screening. *Psychology and Health*, *8*(6), 417–433.

Owens, R. G., Daly, J., Heron, K. and Leinster, S. J. (1987). Psychological and social characteristics of attenders for breast screening. *Psychology and Health*, *1*, 303–313.

OXCHECK, S. G. I. C. R. F. (1995). Effectiveness of health checks conducted by nurses in primary care: Final results in the OXCHECK study. *British Medical Journal*, *310*, 1099–1104.

Panos (1988). *AIDS and the Third World*. London: The Panos Institute.

Panos (1990). *The Third Epidemic: Repercussions and the Fear of AIDS*. London: The Panos Institute.

Parkes, C. M. (1986). *Bereavement: Studies of Grief in Adult Life*. Harmondsworth: Penguin.

Paton, A. (1994). *ABC of Alcohol*. London: BMJ Publishing Group.

Patterson, T. L., Sallis, J. F., Nader, P. R., Rupp, J. W., McKenzie, T. L., Roppe, B. and Bartok, P. W. (1988). Direct observation of physical activity and dietary behavior in a structured environment: Effects of a family based health promotion program. *Journal of Behavioral Medicine*, *11*, 447–458.

Pearson, M. (1986). Racist notions of ethnicity and health. In S. Rodmell and A. Watt (Eds) *The Politics of Health Education*. London: Routledge & Kegan Paul.

Peckham, S. (1993). Preventing unintended teenage pregnancies. *Public Health*, *107*, 125–133.

Pennebaker, J. (1982). *The Psychology of Physical Symptoms*. New York: Springer Verlag.

Perry, S., Jacobsberg, L. B., Fishman, B., Weiler, P. H., Gold, J. W. M. and Frances, A. J. (1992). Relationship over one year between lymphocytes and psychosocial variables among adults with infection by human immuno-deficiency virus. *Archives of General Psychiatry*, *49*(5), 396–401.

Peters, R. K., Moraye, B., Bear, M. S. and Thomas, D. (1989). Barriers to screening for cancer of the cervix. *Preventive Medicine*, *18*, 133–146.

Peterson, L. (1989). Latchkey children's preparation for self-care: Overestimated, under rehearsed and unsafe. *Journal of Clinical Child Psychology*, *18*, 36–43.

Peterson, L., Bartelstone, J., Kern, T. and Gillies, R. (1995a). Parents' social-ization of children's injury prevention – Description and some initial para-meters. *Child Development*, *66*(1), 224–235.

Peterson, L., Gillies, R., Cook, S. C., Schick, B. and Little, T. (1994). Develop-mental patterns of expected consequences for simulated bicycle injury events. *Health Psychology*, *13*(3), 218–223.

Peterson, L., Oliver, K. K., Brazeal, T. J. and Bull, C. A. (1995b). A develop-mental exploration of expectations for and beliefs about preventing bicycle collision injuries. *Journal of Pediatric Psychology*, *20*(1), 13–22.

PHLS (1992). Sexually transmitted diseases in England and Wales, 1981–1990. *Communicable Diseases Report*, *2*, R1–12.

Phoenix, A. (1991). *Young Mothers?* Cambridge: Polity Press.

Pilgrim, D. and Rogers, A. (1995). Mass childhood immunisation: Some ethical doubts for primary health care workers. *Nursing Ethics*, *21*(1), 63–70.

Pillai, V. and Conaway, M. (1992). Immunisation coverage in Lusaka, Zambia: Implications of the social setting. *Journal of Biosocial Science*, *24*(2), 201–209.

Pitts, M. K. and Phillips, K. C. (1991). *The Psychology of Health*. London: Routledge.

Pitts, M. K., McMaster, J. and Wilson, P. (1991). An investigation of pre-conditions necessary for the introduction of a campaign to promote breast self examination amongst Zimbabwean women. *Journal of Applied and Community Psychology*, *1*(1), 33–42.

Pitts, M. K., Bowman, M. and McMaster, J. (1995). Reactions to repeated STD infections: Psychosocial aspects and gender issues in Zimbabwe. *Social Science and Medicine*, *40*(9), 1299–1304.

Pitts, M. K., Burtney, E. and Dobraszczyc, U. (in press). 'There is no shame in it any more'. How providers of sexual health advice view young people's sexuality. *Health Education Research: Theory and Practice*.

Price, R. H. (1986). Stress management programming for worksite health promotion. In *Worksite Health Promotion Resource Guide*. Ann Arbor MI: Michigan Department of Public Health.

Prochaska, J. O. and DiClemente, C. C. (1982). Transtheoretical therapy: Towards a more integrative model of change. *Psychotherapy: Theory, Research and Practice*, *20*, 161–173.

Prochaska, J. O. and DiClemente, C. C. (1983). Stages and processes of self-change of smoking: Toward an integrative model of change. *Journal of Consulting and Clinical Psychology*, *51*, 390–395.

Prochaska, J. O. and DiClemente, C. C. (1992). Stages of change in the modification of problem behaviors. In M. Hersen, R. M. Eisler and P. M. Miller (Eds) *Progress in Behavior Modification* (pp. 184–218). Newbury Park, CA: Sage.

Prochaska, J. O., Redding, C. A., Harlow, L. L., Rossi, J. S. and Velicer, W. F. (1994a). The Transtheoretical Model of Change and HIV Prevention – A Review. *Health Education Quarterly*, *21*(4), 471–486.

Prochaska, J. O., Velicer, W. F., Rossi, J. S., Goldstein, M. G., Marcus, B. H. and Rakowski, W. (1994b). Stages of change and decisional balance for 12 problem behaviors. *Health Psychology*, *13*(1), 39–46.

Pruyn, J., van der Borne, H., de Reuver, R., de Boer, M., Ter Pelkwijk, M. and de Jong, P. (1988). The locus of control scale for cancer patients. *Tijdscrift vour Sociale Gezondhersdszong*, *66*, 404–408.

Quadrel, M. J., Fischoff, B. and Davis, W. (1993). Adolescent (in)vulnerability. *American Psychologist*, *48*(2), 102–116.

Rakowski, W., Dube, C. E., Marcus, B. H., Prochaska, J. O., Velicer, W. F. and Abrams, D. B. (1992). Assessing elements of women's decisions about mammography. *Health Psychology*, *11*(2), 111–118.

Rakowski, W., Fulton, J. P. and Feldman, J. P. (1993a). Women's decision making about mammography – A replication of the relationship between stages of adoption and decisional balance. *Health Psychology*, *12*(3), 209–214.

Rakowski, W., Rimmer, B. and Bryant, S. (1993b). Integrating behavior and intention regarding mammography by respondents in the 1990 National Health interview survey of health promotion and disease prevention. *Public Health Reports*, *108*(5), 605–624

Rakowski, W., Bellis, J. M., Velicer, W. F. and Dube, C. A. (1993c). Smoking status and mammography in a statewide survey. *Addictive Behaviors*, *18*(6), 691–696.

Reading, R., Colver, A., Openshaw, S. and Jarvis, S. (1994). Do interventions that improve immunisation uptake also reduce social inequalities in uptake? *British Medical Journal*, *308*, 1142–1144.

Reddy, C. V. (1989). Parents' beliefs about vaccination. *British Medical Journal*, *299*(6701), 739.

Reed, D. M., LcCroix, A. Z., Karasek, R. A., Miller, D. and MacLean, C. A.

(1989). Occupational strain and the incidence of coronary heart disease. *American Journal of Epidemiology*, *129*, 495–502.

Reid, J. A. (1987). *Survey of Parents' Views on Immunisation*. Mersey Regional Health Authority, Liverpool.

Richmond, R. L. and Anderson, P. (1994). Research in general practice for smokers and excessive drinkers in Australia and the U.K. Interpretation of results. *Addiction*, *89*, 35–40.

Roberts, I. (1995). Injuries to child pedestrians. *British Medical Journal*, *310*, 413–414.

Roden, J. (1992). Childhood immunisation levels in Sydney's western metropolitan region: Parental attitudes and nurses' roles. *Australian Journal of Advanced Nursing*, *9*(3), 18–24.

Rogers, W. (1984). Changing health related attitudes and behavior: The role of preventive health psychology. In J. H. Harvey, E. Maddux, R. P. McGlynn and C. D. Stoltenberg (Eds) *Social Perception in Clinical and Counselling Psychology*. Lubbock, Texas: Texas Technical University Press.

Rose, D. P. (1993). Diet, hormones and cancer. *Annual Review of Public Health*, *14*, 1–17.

Rose, G. (1992). *The Strategy of Preventive Health*. Oxford: Oxford University Press.

Rosenblum, E. H., Stone, E. J. and Skipper, B. E. (1981). Maternal compliance in immunization of preschoolers as related to health locus of control, health value and perceived vulnerability. *Nursing Research*, *30*(6), 337–342.

Rosenstock, I. M. (1966). Why people use health services. *Millbank Memorial Fund Quarterly*, *44*, 94.

Rotter, J. B. (1966). Generalised wxpectancies for internal versus external control of reinforcement. *Psychological Monographs*, *80*, 1–28.

Russell, C. and Schofield, T. (1986). *Where it Hurts: An Introduction to Sociology for Health Workers*. Sydney: Allen & Unwin.

Rutledge, D. N. (1987). Factors related to women's practice of breast self examination. *Nursing Research*, *36*(2), 117–121.

Ryan, W. (1976). *Blaming the Victim*. New York: Vintage Books, Random House.

Saggars, S. and Gray, D. (1991). *Aboriginal Health and Society: The Traditional and Contemporary Aboriginal Struggle for Better Health*. Sydney: Allen & Unwin.

Sallis, J. F., Hovell, M. F. and Hofstetter, C. R. (1992). Predictors of adoption and maintenance of vigorous physical activity in men and women. *Preventive Medicine*, *21*, 237–251.

Sanders, D., Peveler, R., Mant, D. and Fowler, G. (1993). Predictors of successful smoking cessation following advice from nurses in general practice. *Addiction*, *88*, 1699–1705.

Sansom, D., Wakefield, J. and Yule, R. (1970). Cervical cytology in the Manchester region: Changing patterns of response. *The Medical Officer* (June), 357–359.

Sanson-Fisher, R. (1993). Primary and secondary prevention of cancer: Opportunities for behavioural scientists. In S. Maes, H. Leventhal and M. Johnston (Eds) *International Review of Health Psychology* London: John Wiley & Sons.

Sarafino, E. P. (1994). *Health Psychology: Biopsychosocial Interactions* (2nd ed.). New York: John Wiley & Sons.

Scheier, M. F. and Carver, C. S. (1985). Optimism, coping and health: Assessment and implications of generalised outcome expectancies. *Health Psychology*, *4*, 219–247.

Scheier, M. F. and Carver, C. S. (1992). Effects of optimism on psychological and physical well-being: The influence of generalised outcome expectancies on health. *Journal of Personality, 55*, 169–210.

Schleifer, S. J., Keller, S. E., Camerino, M., Thornton, J. C. and Stein, M. (1983). Suppression of lymphocyte stimulation following bereavement. *Journal of American Medical Association, 250*, 374–377.

Schwarzer, R. (1994). Optimism, vulnerability, and self-beliefs as health-related cognitions: A systematic overview. *Psychology and Health, 9*(3), 161–180.

Senior, M. L., New, S. J. and Gatrell, A. C. (1990). The uptake of infant immunisations: Do geographical factors influence attendance? At the Annual Meeting of the Institute of British Geographers. University of Glasgow.

Shaper, A. G. (1990). Alcohol and mortality: A review of prospective studies. *British Journal of Addiction, 85*, 837–847.

Shapiro, S., Venet, W., Strax, P., Venet, L. and Roeser, R. (1985). Selection, follow up and analysis in the Health Insurance Plan study: A randomized trail with breast cancer screening. *National Cancer Institute Monographs, 67*, 65–74.

Sharpe, S. (1987). *Falling for Love: Teenage Mothers Talk*. London: Virago Press.

Sheeran, P., White, D. and Phillips, K. (1991). Premarital contraceptive use: A review of the psychological literature. *Journal of Reproductive and Infant Psychology, 9*, 253–269.

Sheley, J. F. and Lesan, G. T. (1986). Limited impact of the breast self examination movement: A Latin American illustration. *Social Science and Medicine, 23*, 905–910.

Shilts, R. (1987). *And the Band Played On*. Harmondsworth: Penguin.

Siegrist, J. R. P., Junge, A., Cremer, P. and Siedel, D. (1990). Low status control, high effort at work and ischaemic heart disease: Prospective evidence from blue collar men. *Social Science and Medicine, 31*, 1127–1134.

Siegrist, J. R. P., Motz, W. and Strauer, B. E. (1992). The role of hypertension, left ventricular hypertrophy and psychosocial risks in cardiovascular disease: Prospective evidence from blue collar men. *European Heart Journal, 13* (Supplement D), 89–95.

Simpson, N., Lenton, S. and Randall, R. (1995). Parental refusal to have children immunised: Extent and reasons. *British Medical Journal, 310*, 227.

Singleton, V. and Michael, M. (1993). Actor-networks and ambivalence: General practitioners in the UK cervical cancer screening programme. *Social Studies of Science, 23*, 227–264.

Sloan, R. and Gruman, J. (1983). Beliefs about cancer, heart disease and their victims. *Psychological Reports, 52*, 415–424.

Smith, J., Cohen, H. H., Cohen, A. and Cleveland, R. J. (1978). Characteristics of successful safety programs. *Journal of Safety Research, 10*, 67–85.

Smyth, M. and Browne, F. (1992). *General Household Survey, 1990*. London: HMSO.

Sobel, R. (1969). Traditional safety measures and accidental poisoning in children. *Pediatrics, 44* (Supplement), 811–816.

Sontag, S. (1979). *Illness as Metaphor*. New York: Farrar, Strauss & Giroux.

Sontag, S. (1988). *AIDS and its Metaphors*. Harmondsworth: Penguin.

Stainton Rogers, W. (1991). *Explaining Health and Illness: An Exploration of Diversity*. Hemel Hempstead: Harvester Wheatsheaf.

Standing, H. and Kisseka, M. N. (1989). *Sexual Behaviour in Sub-Saharan Africa*. London: Overseas Development Agency.

Stanford, J. (1987). Testicular self examination. *Journal of Advanced Nursing*, *12*, 13–19.

Stanton, A. (1987). Determinance of adherence to medical regimens by hypertensive patients. *Journal of Behavioral Medicine*, *10*, 377–394.

Stedman, Y., Woodman, C. B. J. and Donnelly, B. J. (1995). Is a policy of cervical screening for all women attending a genito-urinary medicine clinic justified? *Journal Public Health Medicine*, *17*(1), 90–92.

Steffen, V. (1990). Men's motivation to perform the testicle self exam: Effects of prior knowledge and an educational brochure. *Journal of Applied Social Psychology*, *20*(8), 681–702.

Steffen, V. and Gruber, V. (1991). Direct experience with a cancer self-exam: Effects on cognitions and behaviors. *The Journal of Social Psychology*, *131*(2), 165–177.

Stehr-Green, P. A., Sprauer, M. A., Williams, W. W. and Sullivan, K. M. (1990). Predictors of vaccination behavior among persons age 65 years and older. *American Journal of Public Health*, *80*(9), 1127–1129.

Stephens, T. (1988). Physical activity and mental health in the United States and Canada: Evidence from four population surveys. *Preventive Medicine*, *17*, 35–47.

Stillman, M. J. (1977). Women's health beliefs about breast cancer and breast self examination. *Nursing Research*, *26*(2), 121–127.

Stone, A. A., Reed, B. R. and Neale, J. M. (1987). Changes in daily event frequency precede episodes of physical symptoms. *Journal of Human Stress*, 70–74.

Stone, A. A., Porter, L. S. and Neale, J. M. (1993). Daily events and mood prior to the onset of respiratory illness episodes: A replication of the 3–5 day 'desirability dip'. *British Journal of Medical Psychology*, *66*(4), 383–394.

Stone, A. A., Neale, J. M., Cox, D. S., Napoli, A., Valdimarsdottir, H. and Kennedy-Moore, E. (1994). Daily events are associated with a secretory immune response to an oral antigen in men. *Health Psychology*, *13*(5), 440–446.

Stone, D. H., Mitchell, S., Packham, B. and Williams, J. (1994a). Prevalence and first-line treatment of diarrhoeal symptoms in the community. *Public Health*, *108*(1), 61–68.

Stroebe, M. S. (1994). The broken heart phenomenon – An examination of the mortality of bereavement. *Journal of Community and Applied Social Psychology*, *4*(1), 47–61.

Stroebe, W. S. and Stroebe, M. S. (1994). *Social Psychology and Health*. Buckingham: Open University Press.

Surry, J. (1979). *Industrial Accident Research*. Toronto: University of Toronto.

Tabar, L., Fagerberg, G., Gad, A., Baldetorp, L., Holmberg, L. H. *et al.* (1985). Reduction in mortality from breast cancer after mass screening with mammography: Randomised trial from the Breast Cancer Screening Working Group of the Swedish National Board of Health and Welfare. *Lancet*, *1*, 829–832.

Tabar, L., Fagerberg, G., Duffy, S. W. and Day, N. E. (1989). The Swedish two-county trial of mammographic screening for breast cancer: Recent results and calculation of benefit. *Journal of Epidemiology and Communications for Health*, *43*, 107–114.

Taylor, R. (1979). Health and class in Australia. *New Doctor*, *13*, 22–28.

Taylor, S. A. (1995). *Health Psychology* (3rd ed.). New York: McGraw Hill.

Terry, D. J., Gallois, C. and McCamish, M. (1993). The Theory of Reasoned Action and health care behaviour. In D. J. Terry, C. Gallois and M. McCamish (Eds) *The Theory of Reasoned Action: Its Application to AIDS-Preventive Behaviour* (pp. 1–29). Oxford: Pergamon Press.

Tesh, S. N. (1988). *Hidden Arguments: Political Ideology and Disease Prevention Policy*. New Brunswick: Rutgers University Press.

Thomson, R. and Halland, J. (1994). Young women and safer (hetero)sex: Context, constraints and strategies. In S. Wilkinson and C. Kitzinger (Eds) *Women and Health: Feminist Perspectives*. Basingstoke: Taylor & Francis.

Tormans, G., Van Damme, P., Carrin, G., Clara, R. and Eylenbosch, W. (1993). Cost effectiveness analysis of prenatal screening and vaccination against hepatitis B virus – The case of Belgium. *Social Science and Medicine, 37*(2), 173–181.

Totman, R., Kiff, J., Reed, S. E. and Craig, J. W. (1980). Predicting experimental colds in volunteers from different measures of recent life stress. *Journal of Psychosomatic Research, 24*, 155–163.

Townsend, J. (1993). Policies to halve smoking deaths. *Addiction, 88*, 43–52.

Townsend, P. and Davidson, N. (Eds) (1982). *Inequalities in Health: The Black Report*. Harmondsworth: Penguin.

Tymstra, T. and Bieleman, B. (1987). The psychosocial impact of mass screening for cardiovascular risk factors. *Family Practice, 4*, 287–290.

Vaile, M. S. B., Calnan, M., Rutter, D. R. and Wall, B. (1993). Breast cancer screening services in three areas: uptake and satisfaction. *Journal of Public Health Medicine, 15*(1), 37–45.

Van Rijn, O. J. L., Bouter, L. M., Kester, A. D. M., Knipschild, P. G. and Meertens, R. M. (1991). Aetiology of burns injuries among children aged 0–4: Results of a case control study. *Burns, 17*, 213–219.

Wadsworth, J., Weelings, K., Johnson, A. M. and Field, J. (1993). Sexual behaviour. *British Medical Journal, 306*, 582–583.

Wall, L. L. (1988). *Hausa Medicine: Illness and Wellbeing in a West African Culture*. Greensboro N.C.: Duke University Press.

Wallace, P., Cutler, S. and Haines, A. (1988). Randomised controlled trial of general practitioner intervention in patients with excessive alcohol consumption. *British Medical Journal, 297*, 663–668.

Wallston, B. S. and Wallston, K. A. (1984). Social psychological models of health behavior. An examination and integration. In A. Baum, S.E. Taylor and J. E. Singer (Eds) *Handbook of Psychology and Health: Volume 4. Social Psychological Aspects of health* (pp. 23–53). Hillsdale, NJ: Lawrence Erlbaum.

Wallston, K. A. (1994). Cautious optimism versus cockeyed optimism. *Psychology and Health, 9*(3), 201–203.

Wallston, K. A., Wallston, B. S. and De Vellis, R. (1978). Development of the multidimensional health locus of control (MHLC) scales. *Health Education Monographs, 6*, 161–170.

Weinstein, N. (1988). The precaution adoption process. *Health Psychology, 11*, 355–386.

Weinstein, N. D. (1993). Testing four competing theories of health-protective behavior. *Health Psychology, 12*(4), 324–333.

Wellings, K. and Bradshaw, S. (1994). First intercourse between men and women. In K. Wellings, J. Field, A. M. Johnson and J. Wadsworth (Eds) *Sexual Behaviour in Britain*. London: Penguin.

Wellings, K., Field, S., Johnson, A. M. and Wadsworth, J. (1994). Studying sexual lifestyles. In K. Wellings, J. Field, A. M. Johnson and J. Wadsworth (Eds) *Sexual Behaviour in Britain*. London: Penguin.

White, E., Urban, N. and Taylor, V. (1993). Mammography utilization, public health impact and cost effectiveness in the United States. *Annual Review of Public Health, 14*, 605–33.

White, G. E. (1995). Older women's attitudes to cervical screening and cervical cancer: A New Zealand experience. *Journal of Advanced Nursing, 24*(4), 659–666.

WHO (1946). *Constitution*. New York: World Health Organisation.

WHO (1986). *The Ottawa Charter for Health Promotion*. Health and Welfare Canada, Ottawa: WHO, Canadian Public Health Association.

WHO (1988). *Promoting Health in the Urban Context* (FADL No. 1). WHO Health Cities. Geneva: World Health Organisation.

Wight, D. (1993). Constraints or cognition? Young men and safer heterosexual sex. In P. Aggleton, P. Davies and G. Hart (Eds) *AIDS, The Second Decade*. Basingstoke: Falmer Press.

Wight, D. (1993). A re-assessment of health education on HIV/AIDS for young heterosexuals. *Health Education Research, 8*(4), 473–483.

Wilkinson, S. and Kitzinger, C. (1993). Whose breast is it any? A feminist consideration of advice and treatment for breast cancer. *Women's Studies International Forum, 16*(3), 229–238.

Wilson, D., Sibanda, B., Mboyi, L., Msimanga, S. and Dube, G. (1990). A pilot study for an HIV prevention programme among commercial sex workers in Bulawayo, Zimbabwe. *Social Science and Medicine, 31*(5), 609–618.

Wilson, D., Lavelle, S., Hood, R., Mavasere, S., Simunyu, E. and Zenda, A. (1991a). Ethnographic and quantitative research to design a community intervention among long distance truckers in Zimbabwe. At *VII International Conference on AIDS*. Florence, Italy, 16–21 June.

Wilson, D., Nyati, B., Nhariwa, M., Lamson, N and Weir, S. (1991b). Programme to reduce HIV transmission among vulnerable groups in Bulawayo, Zimbabwe: Experiences and lessons. In M. A. Mercer and S. J. Scott (Eds) *Tradition and Transition: NGOs Respond to AIDS in Africa* (pp. 65–76). Baltimore: Johns Hopkins University.

Wilson, V. E., Morley, M. C. and Bird, E. I. (1980). Mood profile of marathon runners, joggers and non-exercisers. *Perceptual and Motor Skills, 50*, 117–118.

Winett, R. A., King, A. C. and Altman, D. G. (1989). *Health Psychology and Public Health*. New York: Pergamon Press.

Witte, K., Stokols, D., Ituarte, P. and Schneider, M. (1993). Testing the Health Belief Model in a field study to promote bicycle safety helmets. *Communication Research, 20*(4), 564–586.

Woo, B., Cook, F., Weisberg, M. and Goldman, L. (1985). Screening procedures in an asymptomatic adult: Comparison of physicians' recommendations, patients' desires, published guidelines, and actual practice. *Journal of the American Medical Association, 254*, 1480–1484.

Wood, R. Y. (1994). Reliability and validity of a breast self-examination proficiency rating instrument. *Eval health Prof, 17*(4), 418–435.

Wortel, E., Degeus, G. H., Kok, G. and Vanwoerkum, C. (1994). Injury control in pre-school children – A review of parental safety measures and the behavioural determinants. *Health Education Research, 9*(2), 201–213.

Wortel, E. and Ooijendijk, W. T. M. (1988). *Prevention of Home Related Accidents of Children: Research on Parental Preventive Behavior and Behavioural Determinants.* Leiden: NIPG-TNO.

Wulfert, E. and Wan, C. (1993). Condom use: A self-efficacy model. *Health Psychology, 12*(5), 346–353.

Zapka, J. G. and Mamon, J. A. (1982). Integration of theory, practitioner, standards, literature findings, and baseline data: A case study in planning breast self examination. *Health Education Quarterly, 9*, 330–357.

Zeitlyn, S., & al, e. (1992). Compliance with diptheria, tetanus and pertussis immunisation in Bangladesh. *British Medical Journal, 304*(6827), 606–609.

Zondag, A. and Voorhoeve, H. (1992). Immunisation and nutritional status of under fives in rural Zambia. *Central African Journal of Medicine, 38*(2), 62–66.

Name index

Subject index

abortion, 78
acceptance, 89
access to clinics, 25
accident prevention, 98, 103, 105, 107, 108, 116
accident-prone worker, 116
accidents, 2, 51, 54, 98–100, 105–7, 116, 117; in the elderly, 105
action, 2, 9, 14–17, 26, 35, 42, 48, 49, 53, 76, 84, 90, 99, 104, 107–9, 112, 115, 118, 119, 126
action planning, 14
addiction, 62
adherence, 65. *See* compliance
adolescence, 8
adolescent, 8, 28, 70, 73, 77, 78, 99
adolescent invulnerability, 8, 28
advice, 25, 26, 27, 38, 39, 47, 49, 56, 58, 62, 63, 77, 86, 124
aerobics, 58, 63, 65
Africa, 61, 67, 72, 73, 74, 80, 107, 113, 114, 115
age, 2, 3, 8, 17, 19, 22, 24, 27, 29, 30, 33–42, 45–9, 52, 54, 59, 60, 64, 65, 68, 70–81, 84, 86, 88, 90–2, 96, 98–113, 119, 121–4
aggression, 101
AIDS, 2, 5, 8, 67–70, 73, 79–81, 89, 109, 113–16. *See* HIV
Alameda, 3, 5, 123
alcohol, 4, 51–61, 89, 108; consequences of use, 51; measurement of, 54; Alcohol Use Disorders Identification Test, 55;

CAGE, 54; Michigan Alcoholism Screening Test, 54. *See* drinking
alcohol consumption, 51–57
Alcohol Use Disorders Identification Test, 55
Alcoholics Anonymous, 58
allergies, 125
America, 22, 44, 90, 94, 103, 104, 113, 114. *See* United States
anger, 64, 87, 102, 108
angina, 39. *See* coronary heart disease
animal studies, 83
antibiotic, 26
antibodies, 19, 82, 83, 86, 96
anxiety, 23, 32, 37, 40, 44, 48, 64, 65
apathy, 29
appraisal, 14
arthritis, 61, 83, 84, 116. *See* rheumatiod arthritis
asbestos, 106
Asia, 21, 36, 63, 114
assertiveness, 58, 77
Assessment of Daily Experiences, 94
attitude, 8, 11–13, 22, 26, 30, 36, 45, 73, 75, 77–81, 102, 104
Australia, 23, 25, 56, 61, 78, 79, 104, 119

Bangladesh, 24
behaviour: preventative health, 3; risk, 3
beliefs, 5–8, 15, 17, 22, 24, 36, 45, 49, 61, 64, 73, 78, 81, 115; biomedical, 5; lay/traditional, 5